USING CRISIS INTERVENTION WISELY

USING
CRISIS
INTERVENTION
WISELY

NURSING80 BOOKS, INTERMED COMMUNICATIONS, INC., HORSHAM, PENNSYLVANIA

NURSING80 BOOKS
Publisher: Eugene W. Jackson
Editorial Director: Daniel L. Cheney
Graphics Director: John Isely
Business Manager: Tom Temple

NURSING SKILLBOOK™ SERIES
Editorial staff for this volume:
Book Editor: Jean Robinson
Clinical Editors: Theresa Croushore, RN, Barbara F. McVan, RN
Designers: Linda Jovinelly, Maggie Moyer, Robert Perry
Marginalia Editors: Kathy Carey, Sanford Robinson, Richard West
Copy Editors: Pat Hamilton, Barbara Hodgson
Researcher and Indexer: Vonda Heller
Production Manager: Bernard Haas
Typography Manager: David C. Kosten
Production Assistants: Betty Mancini, Diane Paluba, Doreen Stowers
Artists: Diane Fox, Robert Jackson, Sandra Simms
Photography and Divider Art: Arthur Tress
Cover: Daniel Panachyda

Clinical consultants:

Kristine Kroner, RN, BSN, *Assistant Head Nurse, Surgical Floor, Albert Einstein Medical Center, Philadelphia, Pennsylvania*
Dorothy A. Hyde, RN, MS, CPNA, *Pediatric Nurse Associate, St. Paul-Ramsey Hospital, St. Paul, Minnesota*

Library of Congress Cataloging in Publication Data
Main entry under title:

USING CRISIS INTERVENTION WISELY.
    (Nursing Skillbook series)
    "Nursing79 books."
    Bibliography: p.
    Includes index.
    1. Crisis intervention (Psychiatry)   2. Psychiatric
nursing. [DNLM: 1. Crisis intervention—Nursing texts.
WY87 U85]
RC480.6.U83   616.8'91   79-14825
ISBN 0-916730-15-8

CONTENTS

AUTHORS

Theresa Croushore, formerly a triage nurse in the emergency department of Winter Park Memorial Hospital, Winter Park, Florida, is a clinical editor for *Nursing79* Skillbook series. A graduate of Saint Barnabas Hospital School of Nursing, Minneapolis, Minnesota, and a member of the Emergency Department Nurses' Association, she is author of some of the chapters in this book.

Rosemary Cappelli Johnson is an instructor in nursing at St. Francis Medical Center School of Nursing, Trenton, New Jersey. She received her BSN from Trenton State College, and her MA in nursing education from New York University. She is a member of the American Nurses' Association, and the American Association of Colleges of Nursing.

Kristine Kroner received her BSN from Viterbo College, La Crosse, Wisconsin, and is an assistant head nurse in a surgical unit at Albert Einstein Medical Center, Philadelphia, Pennsylvania.

Betty L. Landon, a graduate of Bellevue School of Nursing, New York City, received her BA from the University of Redlands in Redlands, California, and is studying for her master's degree at Temple University, Philadelphia. She is assistant director of nursing for the critical care and emergency departments at Temple University Hospital.

Lanighta Lewis is a loss prevention representative for the St. Paul Fire and Marine Insurance Company for the state of Florida in Winter Park. A graduate of Gifford Memorial Hospital School of Nursing, Randolph, Vermont, she holds a certificate from the National Alcohol Training Course for Professionals, Washington University, St. Louis, Missouri.

Barbara F. McVan, a graduate of Chestnut Hill Hospital School of Nursing in Philadelphia, is one of the clinical editors of the Nursing Skillbook series, and is author of one of the chapters in this book. She has recently been appointed to the position of clinical director of the upcoming *Nursing79* Photobook Series.

Patricia Sue Sharer, a staff nurse in the emergency department of the University of California, San Francisco, is a graduate of Mount Carmel Hospital School of Nursing, Columbus, Ohio.

Barbara C. Stiteler is a graduate of Abington Memorial Hospital School of Nursing, Abington, Pennsylvania. She received her BA from Antioch University, Philadelphia, and is self-employed as a nursing consultant.

Carmen Germaine Warner, a consultant on social and domestic violence, is a graduate of Northwestern Hospital School of Nursing, Minneapolis, Minnesota. She received her BSN and PHN from San Diego State University, and her MSN from the University of San Diego, California. Her memberships include the American Nurses' Association, National League of Nursing, American Public Health Association, Emergency Department Nurses' Association, and the American Society for Training and Development.

FOREWORD

WHAT'S YOUR ROLE in psychologic crisis intervention? If you're like most nurses, you probably feel a little uncertain in crisis situations because you don't know how to help. You know that some crises can be prevented and some are part of living. But, as a staff nurse, you're not sure which are which— or what to do about them.

That's why I'm so pleased to introduce this clearly written, well-designed Skillbook. Not only will it help clear up some of the misconceptions you may have about psychologic crisis, but it'll teach you how to intervene effectively.

In Chinese literature, the words *crisis* and *opportunity* are represented by the same symbol. And in most cases, your daily nursing practice supports this concept: crisis and opportunity do occur simultaneously. For example, the crises experienced by patients and their families present them with opportunities for growth, and you with opportunities for caring, helping, and supporting. The crises experienced by you and your co-workers create similar opportunities; everyone involved in the situation has a chance to grow personally as well as professionally.

To help you gain new insights about crisis intervention, as well as review the basics, this Skillbook is divided into three sections: *Coping with Crisis*; *Helping the Patient and His Family in Crisis*; and *Helping Health-Care Professionals in Crisis*.

Using numerous examples, the first section defines exactly what's meant by both situational and maturational crises and describes what happens when a person's equilibrium is thrown off balance. Then it explains specifically how you can help, even without specialized training in crisis intervention.

Do you know when a person's truly in crisis? You will, if you read this book carefully. Without resorting to clinical jargon, it'll tell you exactly how to assess the three balancing factors that keep a patient's equilibrium on an even keel.

You can then apply these assessment skills to all the crises discussed in this book, from rape to professional burnout. And you'll learn how to intervene effectively, thereby alleviating the crisis or preventing it completely.

One of the things I like best about this Skillbook is its scope. Instead of limiting itself to the crises experienced by patients and their families, it discusses the problems of health professionals, too.

We nurses, like everyone else, have crises occurring in our lives. But in many cases, we deny them, thus ignoring our own personal needs. How foolish this is. As health-care professionals dedicated to helping others, we must also attend to the problems afflicting us. We must prevent personal crises from destroying our capacity to help others.

Helping others, as well as helping ourselves, is what good nursing's all about. But to fulfill this obligation, we need the practical advice of those who really work with patients in crisis, not the platitudes of those who only theorize. That's what makes this Skillbook a standout among books on crisis intervention. Throughout its chapters, it offers the following: conversation charts that contrast nontherapeutic remarks with therapeutic; referral tips, explaining when and where to refer specific crisis patients; a self-assessment questionnaire that'll help you determine your goals; and a feature demonstrating how to protect yourself from a suddenly combative patient.

Suppose you're a supervisor? Or a staff nurse with leadership potential? This Skillbook will teach you how to cope with the unit crises triggered by the daily stresses of patient care. It'll help you deal with the problems of understaffing, personality conflicts, and policy changes. It'll also tell you how to cope with the loss of a key staff member, as well as how to introduce a new one.

One look at the contents of this Skillbook will show you how complete it is. Almost every psychologic crisis you'll see in an average hospital or clinic is represented here: child abuse, unexpected death, drug and alcohol abuse, temporary confusion, and attempted suicide. Within each chapter, you'll find additional features; for example, one on how to help the battered wife, one on how to comfort the parents after crib death (SIDS), and one on how to ease the stress of a patient on a respirator.

Finally, this Skillbook tells how to prevent crises from recurring. Crisis intervention is based on the premise that everyone has some resources to draw on, no matter how bleak the situation. As a short-term therapist, you can help the crisis patient and his family reestablish balance in their lives. And you can help them grow by reinforcing positive coping mechanisms. Can anything be more satisfying? I doubt it. Just knowing that you said and did the right thing in a crisis situation is enough.

—GLORIA FERRARO DONNELLY, RN, MSN
Nursing Consultant

COPING
WITH CRISIS

"Stress by itself isn't crisis—not even severe stress. Nor is a stressful event like job loss or illness a crisis, although such an event may precipitate a crisis."

"No two persons see a stressful event in exactly the same way; nor does one person always see it the same as he did before."

"Never see yourself as a problem-solver. When you intervene in a crisis, you don't attempt to solve the patient's problems for him; he must do that on his own."

"Always include the patient when you're making plans. No matter how good your intentions look on his care plan, you won't get him to cooperate with them if he doesn't want to."

1

Recognizing people in crisis

BY ROSEMARY JOHNSON, RN, BSN, MA

YOU HEAR A LOT about crisis intervention these days. But do you know what it is, exactly, and when it's truly needed? How do you define the word crisis? The same as other nurses in your unit? Take time to ask a few of them. You may be surprised at their answers.

For example, one nurse we asked for this Skillbook defined crisis as "severe stress." Another saw the crisis patient as a "patient in trouble." Still another called crisis "an unexpected occurrence." And one said the crisis patient "can't adapt to hospitalization."

Understanding the terms

Do you agree with these definitions? Chances are, you think that they're partly right, but you suspect none describes crisis exactly.

Defined more precisely, psychologic crisis occurs when a person under severe stress needs immediate help—or intervention—to restore his equilibrium.

Stress by itself isn't crisis—not even severe stress. Nor is a stressful event like job loss or illness a crisis, although such an event may precipitate a crisis. In some cases, an event that

Steps leading to crisis
- The patient's faced with a stressful situation.
- He tries to cope with the stress and fails.
- His frustration makes him angry or depressed.
- He can't overcome his frustrations and he loses his equilibrium.
- He goes into crisis.

triggers a crisis in one person may scarcely even affect another. So much depends on the person's feelings about the situation, as well as his ability to cope with it at that time. The same situation occurring at another time in the person's life may not upset him unduly.

What leads to crisis

Let's examine the components of a crisis more closely. As you know, no one has a life devoid of daily problems or stresses. Each person strives to maintain his equilibrium in an environment that's alternately friendly, hostile, or a combination of both.

When something interferes with a person's ability to maintain his equilibrium, he feels threatened. In some cases, he may even feel threatened by something he *anticipates*, for example, impending surgery. He may also feel threatened by something he *imagines* has occurred, as he might when he fears having cancer.

Keep in mind that a person must perceive an event or situation as a stress before it can threaten his equilibrium. For example, imagine an elderly patient who suffers from claustrophobia. Having the curtain drawn around his bed may cause him severe stress. To the patient in the next bed, however, a drawn curtain may afford comfort.

When coping fails

Once a person perceives an event as stressful, of course he experiences tension. Because tension causes him discomfort, he tries to reduce it with his usual coping mechanisms—talking to a friend, eating, playing tennis, or whatever. If these don't work—or are somehow unavailable to him—his tension remains unrelieved. It may even increase with prolonged stimulation from the stress.

Now a new danger presents itself. As tension mounts and coping efforts continue to fail, he becomes frustrated—which worsens his growing distress. In some cases, this may deplete his coping energies so quickly that—left on his own—he can no longer deal constructively with his own problem.

That person is in crisis and needs immediate help or intervention to restore his equilibrium. Such help is short-term and focuses on solving the immediate problem. *Crisis intervention is not long-term therapy for severe mental illness.*

"Watch for the patient faced with a stressful situation. He may take the steps which lead to crisis."

Classifying crises

Most authorities classify crises as either situational or maturational.
• Situational crises result from sudden events like hospitalization, loss of a job or a loved one, or natural disaster.
• Maturational crises relate to stages in a person's normal development like puberty, marriage, menopause, or old age.

Most of the crises you'll encounter in a hospital are situational ones, but don't overlook the possibility that a maturational crisis is compounding the problem.

Crisis checklist

To differentiate between a patient who's effectively coping with severe stress, one who's heading for a crisis, and one who's already in crisis, complete the following steps:
• Investigate unusual behavior.
• Look for a triggering event.
• Determine how involved the patient is with his problem.
• Assess his balancing factors. To understand these better, see the illustration on page 22.

Let's examine these steps in your assessment more closely, beginning with the patient's behavior, which serves as a stress barometer.

Investigate the unusual

Being hospitalized, or bringing a loved one to the hospital, is a stressful event for most people. However, no one can predict how each person will perceive the event, or if he can cope with it successfully. He may do reasonably well at first, then falter under added stress. Or he may start out poorly, then develop new coping mechanisms that'll help him adapt to his situation.

You'll get your first impression of your patient's coping abilities when you do your initial assessment. At that time, watch for physical and psychologic clues that he's under severe stress.

Investigate anything unusual. For example, is the patient extremely quiet? Does he talk incessantly? Is he fearful? What about physical signs and symptoms. Are his hands cold and clammy? Does he complain of indigestion? Is he breathing irregularly?

Try to find out what's normal for your patient, so you don't reach any false conclusion about his stress level. Just because a patient's taciturn doesn't mean he's suffering severe stress. Ask him or his family if he's always been like that.

He may be upset by something you're doing (and can quickly remedy); for example, asking him a lot of personal questions in front of his roommate. Or rushing him for answers. Or not taking time to make him comfortable.

Try to understand why your patient's behaving the way he is, and strive to accept him. Any negative feelings you show toward him will add to his stress. What's more, you can't assess a patient's stress level accurately if your own feelings interfere. You're sure to react differently, even though you may not realize it.

Crisis: Is it or isn't it?

Recognizing the person in crisis isn't always easy. Since you can't get inside his mind, you can't tell how realistically he perceives a situation or if he can cope with it successfully. No two persons see a stressful event in exactly the same way; nor does one person always see it the same as he did before.

So how can you determine if a person's coping mechanisms are exhausted? In this chapter, I'll give you some general guidelines for an accurate assessment. Then in subsequent chapters, you'll learn how to apply these guidelines to specific cases. You'll even learn how to recognize crisis in yourself or in other nurses.

The last straw

Remember this: A true crisis is always precipitated by a stressful event that's occurred—most likely—within the past 2 weeks. Of course, such an event may not be the only threat to the patient's equilibrium recently, but *it will be the triggering factor*. To him, it's "the last straw"—the event that throws him into crisis. To others, it may seem rather trivial because they perceive it in a different way.

To illustrate, let's go back to the claustrophobic patient who's admitted to the hospital for a physical disorder. From the moment he arrived, his equilibrium has been in jeopardy. Besides the usual stresses connected with illness and hospitalization, he's felt threatened by situations that most patients accept routinely: for example, riding in an elevator, undergoing various diagnostic tests, waiting alone in a small examination room, and having the curtain drawn around his bed. To make matters worse, he's no longer in control of the situation as he was at home. Many of his usual coping mechanisms aren't available to him now. Then, without preliminary warning, you raise the side rails on his bed. Is it any wonder that this additional stress panics him? This patient could be thrown into crisis over such a trivial incident.

You may possibly prevent such a crisis by recognizing the danger signs. These present themselves in your assessment, which is applicable to anyone in stress—no matter what the setting.

When feelings are a problem
One of your biggest challenges in crisis intervention is learning to resolve your feelings toward patients who make you feel uneasy. Whether you accept or disregard your feelings, they do influence your nursing care. For example:
• How do you feel about the uncooperative patient? Do you avoid trying to understand him? Does he make you uncomfortable? Do you give him less attention than you give other patients? He may be in crisis and need your help more than anyone. What do you expect of yourself in this situation? Discussing the problem with other nurses may help. Perhaps they can suggest ways to relieve his stress and make your job easier.
• How do you feel about the patient who's crying? Do you ignore him? Avoiding someone in tears is a learned response based on embarrassment. Instead, draw on your natural empathy. Ask yourself why he's crying. Determine whether it's an effective coping mechanism. Say: "I'll give you some time to yourself and then come back." Watch for a patient holding back tears. Maybe he's only waiting to be alone. Find him some privacy. By listening to the patient in tears or providing support or solitude, you can help ease his stress and perhaps avert a crisis.

IN CRISIS OR NOT IN CRISIS?

Carol Dean, who is 13 weeks pregnant, moves into town. Her husband, Max. One day while she's alone, she develops profuse vaginal bleeding and drives to the emergency department of your hospital.

"Max wants this baby so much," she says fearfully. "I hope I don't lose it." Since she has no local obstetrician, the E.D. doctor and then a gynecologist examine her. They advise her to have a D&C and begin explaining the procedure. Carol withdraws into silence. When you approach her with the surgical consent form, she stares at the wall and drops the pen you give her. How do you assess her situation:

Follow the guidelines you'll find on page 22.

• Does she have a realistic perception of the event? No. Because of emotional distress she fails to understand exactly what's happening.

• Are those she relies on for support present? No.

• Are her coping mechanisms working? You're not sure. But it's clear she can't function.

Weighing all factors, you determine she's in crisis.

You contact her husband, who immediately comes to the hospital. After talking with the doctor, Max and Carol prepare for her surgery and begin the grieving process together.

Lynn and Bob Wilson are expecting their first child. When Lynn develops spotting in her 14th week, her doctor explains that slight bleeding is fairly common and asks her to keep him informed. A few days later, the bleeding gets worse. Bob takes Lynn to meet her doctor at the emergency department where you work. He examines her and recommends a D&C. When you interview Lynn, you notice her clenched fists and tearful eyes. In a tremulous voice, she asks you how long the procedure will take and how long she'll be hospitalized.

Is Lynn in crisis? You assess her situation:

• Does she have a realistic perception of the event? Yes, she's prepared for the abortion and seems to know what to expect.

• Are those she relies on for support present? Yes, her husband and regular doctor are there.

• Are her coping mechanisms working? Apparently. Even though she's in stress, she seems to be dealing effectively with the prospect of abortion.

You decide Lynn Wilson's not in crisis.

However, she'll still need your support to help maintain her equilibrium through the acute phase of grief.

To illustrate, imagine yourself interviewing a mother who has severely abused her own child. Would you care as much about her stress level as you would if her child were dying from leukemia? You must examine your own feelings and consider how they'll affect the conclusions you draw about a patient. You may have to ask someone else to do the interview, to insure its accuracy.

Take care to exclude irrelevant data when you're doing your assessment. For example, don't assume a patient can cope constructively with depression because he's a psychologist. And don't assume a nurse-patient can cope with a serious illness like multiple sclerosis just because she's a nurse.

Keep your assessment ongoing. Make every encounter you have with each patient a meaningful one. Don't rush in and out of his room without speaking; take a minute to talk to him. Do you detect signs of increasing stress? Does he have a problem?

Remember this: A patient who says he has a problem deserves your attention, no matter *how insignificant that problem may seem to you*. When someone's in severe stress, even a trivial incident can throw him into crisis.

Be a good listener. Follow up verbal and nonverbal clues with reflective questions. Or say something like "You don't seem as relaxed today," to a patient who suddenly becomes very uncooperative. In Chapter 2, you'll find further guidelines for communicating with the patient who's in stress. But here I'm just discussing your assessment of his stress level; not your intervention.

Do physical or psychologic clues suggest your patient's in severe stress? Don't just assume stress is in back of every unusual sign or symptom—even if you know your patient's unduly anxious. Always investigate each clue carefully to make sure it's not caused by some physical disorder or drug toxicity. Your patient may develop a new condition that requires the doctor's attention.

Recognizing crisis signposts
Now let's suppose you've completed the first step in your assessment. You've determined that your patient's in severe stress, but you're still not sure if he's in crisis. If he's in crisis, he'll need your immediate intervention. He'll be panicked, and no longer capable of coping constructively with his own problem.

Working swiftly, continue your assessment. Find out the answers to these questions:

• *Has something happened within the past few weeks to trigger this patient's undue stress?* Remember, a triggering event may seem quite trivial to you, but it's of critical importance to the patient. To find out about it, you may have to ask him a direct question: "Has anything particularly upsetting happened to you within the past few weeks?" If he can't reply, ask his family. Or just ask any of them to describe the past few weeks in detail.

• *How involved is this patient with his problem?* Chances are, he thinks and talks of nothing else if he's in true crisis. He may not even groom himself as he did before or care what day it is. You'll discover this quickly when you look in on him, or compare notes with other nurses. Or you can ask his family if he's seemed preoccupied with anything lately.

Nursing tip: Anytime you notice a patient becoming increas-

Crisis teamwork
Accurate crisis assessment isn't easy. No matter how good a nurse you are, you never know exactly what a patient's thinking or feeling. But a team approach can help. When a patient seems particularly upset, pool the information you've gathered on him. One way to do this is through formal staff conferences, but sometimes problems can't wait. Seek out nurses and other hospital staff members whose opinions you respect. Tell them what you've observed and ask what they think. Remember: The more viewpoints you get on a particular patient's problems, the more effectively you can help him.

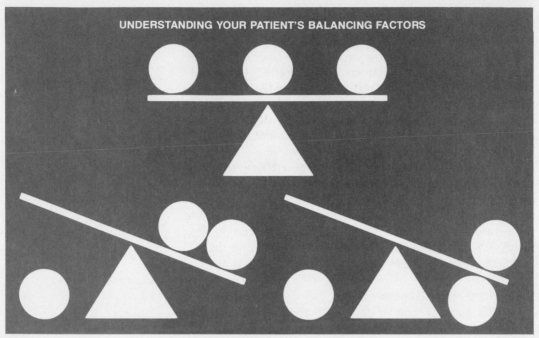

UNDERSTANDING YOUR PATIENT'S BALANCING FACTORS

During stress, the three balancing factors that help a person maintain his equilibrium are: his realistic perception of the stressful event, his emotional supports, and his coping mechanisms. If all three factors are present, as they are in the top figure, your patient will probably deal with stress adequately. If only two factors are present, he may have difficulty. If he has only one balancing factor, chances are he'll soon be in crisis.

ingly preoccupied with a conflict or problem in his life, be sure to document it. This will alert you and other staff members to the stress he's under and may help you prevent a crisis.

Check those balancing factors
Do your new findings reinforce your worry that the patient's in crisis? Check his balancing factors as the final step in your assessment. To do this properly, ask yourself:

• *Has he perceived the stressful event that's occurred to him realistically? Or has he misinterpreted it because of fear or ignorance?* For example, suppose you're caring for a patient with newly diagnosed diabetes. If he's convinced his disease will turn him into a helpless invalid, he's perceiving his stress unrealistically. He needs your immediate help: patient teaching.

• *Does he have adequate emotional supports? Are they available to him now?* Try to find out who he "leans on" when he's in stress. If he's like most of us, he depends on family members or friends for emotional support. If he has none, or if they're unavailable to him because he's in the hospital, he's missing an important balancing factor that he needs to fight stress.

Chances are, you learned what emotional supports your patient has when you took his history. Check his initial assessment form for the information or ask him directly. *Nursing tip:* To find out how to enter information of this type on an assessment form, read the Skillbook *Documenting Patient Care Responsibly*.

• *How does he usually cope with stress? Are these coping mechanisms available to him now?* For example, he may manage stress in his life by overeating, drinking, or smoking. Or he may withdraw from contact with others, seek out certain friends, or yell at his family. Ask your patient or his family what he usually does when he's feeling upset. Has he been deprived of an effective coping mechanism because of hospital routine? Perhaps you can alter his routine slightly to provide him this hedge against stress. Or you can help him find some new coping mechanisms that will substitute temporarily for the old ones.

Important: Before you decide that your patient isn't coping adequately, ask yourself what you've based that decision on. Are you expecting him to cope the way you'd cope or another patient copes? Remember, he's an individual and he has his own ways to manage stress. Just because he doesn't react the way you would doesn't mean he's not coping successfully. Give him a chance before you intervene.

No easy conclusion
You've come to the end of your assessment. Is your patient in actual crisis, requiring your immediate intervention? Or is he holding his own with severe stress, requiring nothing beyond quality nursing care and your usual empathy.

Don't rush to intervene in a patient's problems if he doesn't need you. Chances are, if he has two or more balancing factors present, he isn't in crisis. But that doesn't mean he won't go into crisis later; his balancing factors may shift abruptly.

Important: No matter how carefully you follow the guidelines I've given you in this chapter, you won't always find it easy to tell if a patient's in true crisis. For example, you may think he can't cope with his problems because he suddenly

Now you see it, now you don't
Are all your patients in crisis? Or none of them? Chances are, if you think either extreme is true, *your* perception is unrealistic. You may be getting too involved with your patients or else denying their problems. Consider the cases of these two nurses:

Carrie Jackson, who's regarded as calm and collected, rarely sees signs of impending crisis in her patients. In her opinion, almost all of them cope well with their illness and hospitalization. Carrie believes this good record shows she's fulfilled her nursing goals.

Linda Meyers, on the other hand, sees crises everywhere. She believes each of her patients has a bigger problem than the doctor realizes. Her objective is to uncover it. Looking for problems has become as important to her as solving them.

Neither of these nurses makes *objective* patient assessments. By basing their treatments on inaccurate assessments, they're compounding, not easing, their patients' problems.

refuses visitors; when in reality, he needs that temporary solitude to "think things through."

When you're in doubt, ask the patient. Say something like: "This last bit of news has really been upsetting, hasn't it. How are you holding up?" A question like this shows you care and gives him an opportunity to tell you about his feelings. It may even help him sort through the stressful events that have occurred and see them in a new perspective.

Follow up your question by asking him what he's been doing to relieve the stress he feels. You may be surprised how well he's coping with it—or you may learn he can't cope, and no longer wants to. Asking him how he relieves stress has another value. You'll be ready if these coping mechanisms suddenly aren't available to him, which could throw him into crisis.

Keep a close watch
Stay alert. Continue to assess his emotional status, considering each step carefully. Watch for signs of increasing stress, as well as situations that may serve as the triggering event.

In Chapter 2, I'll discuss how you can avert crisis by replacing a missing balancing factor, or strengthening a weak one. You can do much to relieve severe stress if you recognize it and accept the causes behind it.

Read the next chapter carefully, so you have a good foundation for the rest of this book. Then go on to the remaining chapters, where you'll learn more about some of the specific stresses that can threaten a person's equilibrium—and what you can do about them.

2

Applying crisis intervention techniques

BY ROSEMARY JOHNSON, RN, BSN, MA

THE PERSON IN CRISIS: Who is he? From Chapter 1, you learned that he's more than someone in severe stress. He's someone who can no longer constructively cope with the problem he's facing. For the patient dying from cancer, that problem might be loss of good health. For the patient who's had a radical mastectomy, it might be loss of self-esteem.

A crisis state is so intolerable that no one can stay in it indefinitely. One way or another—usually within 6 weeks—the person will end his mental anguish. With proper intervention, he'll hopefully resolve the situation in some positive way—solve the problem or adapt to it. But—with or without intervention—he may resolve it in some negative way—commit suicide, become addicted to alcohol, or develop mental illness.

By knowing the right way to intervene, you'll give the involved person a better chance to pull out of his crisis successfully. But, if you're like many nurses, you find crisis situations scary. You're not sure what to do about them and you don't know if you can cope.

Read this chapter. Chances are, it'll answer a lot of the questions you have on crisis intervention: For example, how

First impressions
How a person first reacts to shocking news can mislead you. He may be so stunned that, unthinkingly, he makes a sense-less or callous-sounding remark.

For example, consider the young woman whose first reaction to her mother's death is: "Well, I guess that means my vacation's off."

Or the patient who requires surgery may try to delay the emotional distress he antici-pates, by refusing to sign a surgical consent form.

Don't try to determine a per-son's stress level from such behavior. The immediate emo-tional response of a person facing great stress may not ac-curately reflect how he'll react and cope later.

to establish rapport with an unfamiliar patient; when to make a referral; how to help the patient who refuses help; and how to suggest alternate ways to cope with a situation.

Understanding your role

To effectively intervene in a crisis, you must use the nursing process. Throughout this chapter, I'll discuss each step in detail, but basically it means you must:

• Assess the patient to see if he's really in crisis.

• Identify his most pressing problem—no matter what it is—and provide immediate relief.

• Set goals (both short- and long-term) and plan interventions that will restore the patient's ability to cope constructively with the situation. Include him in your plans.

• Implement those plans, involving supportive family mem-bers and friends.

• Evaluate what you've done to determine if goals were ac-complished. Revise plans, if necessary, keeping in mind that long-term goals may require long-term therapy.

Most importantly, *never see yourself as a problem-solver.* When you intervene in a crisis, you don't attempt to solve the patient's problems for him; he must do that on his own. Suc-cessful intervention simply helps the patient gain a new per-spective on the situation. Then he can find constructive ways to cope with it, and, eventually, a solution.

First things first

Since I already discussed how to determine if someone's in crisis in Chapter 1, let's go immediately to the next step: identifying and relieving the patient's most pressing problem.

To illustrate, think back to the claustrophobic patient in that chapter. From the time of admission, his stress level escalated rapidly. Then he went into a full-blown crisis when the nurse raised his side rails.

What's his most pressing problem at that point? His diffi-culties adjusting to hospitalization? No, it's the raised side rails, because that's what triggered his panic. Before you can help him adjust to hospitalization, you must do something about his immediate problem. Lower both side rails, or at least one of them.

Stay with him after that so you can establish a rapport that'll help you discover what's behind his crisis. And you can plan

"How a person first reacts to shocking news can mislead you. His immediate emotional response may not accurately reflect how he'll react and cope later."

Do you think one of your patients may soon go into crisis? To help prevent it, you may have to violate his confidence.

Consider the case of Mrs. Campbell, who faces a possible radical mastectomy. As you discuss it, she says, "Don't call my family now. I don't want them to know." What do you do?

• Ask yourself: Is this patient saying one thing and meaning the opposite? Remember, a patient may tell you something "in confidence" *hoping* you'll tell others. To clarify her intentions, ask: "What will happen if they know?"

• Call the family member listed as next of kin. Explain that Mrs. Campbell asked you not to call, but you felt someone should know her situation. Don't tell him what to do. After you relate the facts, he can proceed as he thinks best.

• Tell Mrs. Campbell what you've done and why. Honesty is essential for further rapport.

• Be present, or at least available, when the family comes to see the patient.

• Always document when you've discussed the patient's condition with the family.

further interventions to relieve much of the stress he feels from hospitalization. (Don't try to cure his claustrophobia. Crisis intervention is short-term help, not long-term therapy for deep-seated problems.)

Important: When you sense an impending crisis—or know that one exists—don't waste precious time trying to thoroughly analyze the situation. Calm the patient as quickly as possible. Keep him from hurting himself and others. (For tips on how to deal with the combative patient, see pages 82 to 85.)

Remember, a person in crisis can be very susceptible to suggestions. So use your authority to stop harmful behavior; don't wait for him to make a decision. Issue firm directives like "Sit down," "Drop that knife," or "Get back in your bed." But try not to sound tyrannical, and *never show your alarm*.

Does the patient show signs of being suicidal or homicidal? Get psychiatric help for him *immediately;* don't try to deal with these problems on your own. (For specific guidelines on how to do this, see Chapter 6.)

Make the connection

Now that you've relieved some of the intense anxiety your patient felt at the onset of his crisis, stay with him. Try to establish an immediate "connection" with him; you'll need good rapport to plan and carry out your interventions.

Never expect this step to be easy, even when you know your patient well. You may discover that he's become disoriented since you talked to him last and won't even remember who you are. And if you've never met him before, your job may be doubly difficult. You won't know what he's like in a normal situation, and you may have no one nearby to check with.

Here are some tips that'll help you establish rapport with an unfamiliar patient:

• Decide what you think is his most striking characteristic *at that time.* For example, say "Your hands seem very cold and wet, Mr. Johnson." Just indicating you've noticed shows you're trying to tune into him.

• Give him a chance to respond to your statement. Hopefully, he'll reach out with his own attempt to establish rapport. Be quiet and listen.

Caution: Always investigate striking characteristics that may be caused by physical disorders. For example, don't assume a patient is hyperventilating because he's in severe stress. He may have a respiratory disorder that needs immediate attention.

Knowing what to say

Are the lines of communication open? Strive to keep them open while you get at the patient's problem. Try to discover what's causing his crisis by encouraging him with leading statements, asking therapeutic questions, and listening to his answers. The list below contains general guidelines for how to talk to patients in severe stress. (For more *specific* examples of good and bad responses to your patient's statements, see page 30.)

Here are the guidelines:

• Don't tack labels on your patient. For example, never say "You are a very dependent person, Mrs. Miller." That's being judgmental and immediately puts your patient on the defensive. Instead, say something like, "You seem to rely on your daughter for a lot of things." That's just something you've observed, not something you're being critical about.

• Eliminate vague replies by asking who, what, when, and where. Be careful starting questions with why. Don't let it mean "How come you're having this difficulty?" or "What makes you act like this?"

• Avoid using the pronoun "they," because it's nonspecific. If your patient says things like *"They don't like me"* or *"They don't understand,"* ask him to tell you who he means. Keep the patient from speaking in generalities.

• Help him relive situations by asking him to describe events, feelings, and people in detail. Relate these descriptions to the present to help him understand the connection.

• Give the patient a chance to spontaneously offer information. Don't torment him with a relentless barrage of questions. Guide the conversation; don't *pursue* it.

Watch for contradictory clues

As the patient talks, you're picking up verbal clues to how he feels. But watch also for his nonverbal messages—or what's commonly called his body language. Do his verbal and nonverbal messages contradict each other? Ask him about it.

For example: Suppose you're caring for a patient with a colostomy. He repeatedly assures you he's having no difficulty

Crisis as crossroads

A crisis is, in effect, a crossroads. The patient can take either a path that leads to growth or one that leads to defeat.

By making a constructive effort to resolve his crisis, the patient will benefit from the process and grow. Even an unsuccessful attempt can help: By learning what doesn't work, he can better understand his problems and improve his chances of future success.

However, when the patient makes repeated ineffective attempts—or no attempts at all—to end his crisis, he may lose hope. The result may be disastrous: drug or alcohol addiction, total mental disability, suicide, or homicide.

Remember: You may never see the outcome of a patient's crisis. This makes the early stages—when you're helping him gain direction—that much more important.

CRISIS INTERVENTION THROUGH CONVERSATION

Often simple conversation with a patient in crisis is the best way to understand his particular needs. However, if you're not careful you can unwittingly block important communication by saying the wrong thing at the wrong time. Below you'll find specific examples of "do's and don'ts" in therapeutic conversation.

GENERAL GUIDELINES	WHEN HE SAYS:	DON'T SAY:	SAY:
Don't be judgmental. It discredits the patient's feelings.	"I hate my doctor."	"You shouldn't say things like that."	"What bothers you about him?"
Don't impose your morals on others.	"There's no God."	"That's awful. Don't say things like that."	"When did you start to feel that way? Tell me what happened?"
Empathize; don't sympathize.	"Boy, everything's going wrong."	"You poor thing. That's too bad."	"You feel things are pretty rough now? What things?"
Don't encourage scapegoating.	"This accident is all my parents' fault."	"They *have* caused you problems" or "Things like that happen."	"Tell me how your parents are involved."
Don't try to solve the patient's problems. To grow, he must deal with them on his own.	"So, what should I do?"	"I'll tell you what *I'd* do…".	"What are your choices? Let's talk about each."
Emphasize positive features of behavior.	"I can never rest because my roommate talks all the time."	"If it bothers you, why didn't you say something sooner?"	"Sometimes it takes real courage to mention things like that."
Avoid making threatening statements.	"I am a messenger from another world."	"You need a psychiatrist."	"I'm concerned about you."
Don't negate feelings or bait the patient into fulfilling his statements.	"I want to kill myself."	"Oh, you don't mean that."	"Do you think suicide is your only choice?"
Don't make false promises.	"I know I'll never walk again."	"Everything will turn out all right."	"That must be a scary feeling."
Don't imply that you know everything.	"I feel terrible."	"I know exactly how it is."	"Describe your feelings."

adjusting to his changed body image, but he looks away every time you change his dressing. Don't ignore what his actions tell you. Instead, say something like "You don't seem very comfortable with your stoma. You looked away when I uncovered it."

Get at the problem

As soon as you've established rapport with the patient in crisis, try to identify his problem. To do this, ask him what he thinks it is—and how it's affecting his life. If he can tell you, summarize the problem for him in his own words.

Never assume a patient can readily identify his own problem. If he can't, don't press him. Instead, start talking about the ways he normally copes with problems in his life. Then try to find out when these coping mechanisms failed. Determining the time when this happened may help you pinpoint the problem.

Let's say the patient identifies his problem. Encourage him to explore *every facet* of it. For example, suppose you're talking to a man whose son was killed in a hunting accident. Losing a loved one may not be his *entire* problem. He may also feel guilty about the accident, because he failed to teach the boy proper safety habits.

Here's another important reminder: Don't believe everything you hear. Just because a patient tells you what's bothering him doesn't mean that information is accurate. For example, imagine you're caring for a 60-year-old woman with a fractured hip. When you try to find out what's behind her mounting distress, she says: "I have a sister with a bad heart condition at home, and now there's no one to care for her." Check into the situation carefully before you identify this as her problem. She may be thinking about a relative who died years ago.

Planning further interventions

Have you identified the patient's problem? No matter how you feel about it, try to accept it from his point of view. Indicate you want to help him. Then include him in your plans; don't try to solve the problem by yourself.

Begin by taking a close look at his balancing factors to see where they're weak or absent (see Chapter 1). With the patient's participation, think of ways you can strengthen them. Ask yourself:

Ending conversations gracefully

What do you say to the patient who seems to want to talk forever? Don't let him become too dependent on you. When you enter his room, tell him "I've got ten minutes to talk with you." Let him know you have other responsibilities. If the conversation's becoming repetitive, say so: "We've been over this before. Let's think awhile about what we've discussed. I'll come back at 4 o'clock and we'll talk again." Keep your promise. Remember: Just because a patient wants to take up your whole day talking, doesn't mean he needs to. Try to recognize the difference.

Crisis intervention through physical response
How can you effectively modify your patient's behavior? Consciously try to respond with opposite actions. For example, when a patient:
• talks too fast, too loudly, or stiltedly you should
Speak slowly, softly, and in easily understood terms.
• paces
Sit still.
• gestures excessively
Hold your hands loosely in your lap.
• averts his gaze
Maintain eye contact.
• sits rigidly, seems tense, or anxious
Be relaxed, patient.

• Does this patient need additional patient teaching to correct unrealistic perceptions?

• Does he need additional support systems? Or replacements for missing ones?

• Does he need help finding alternate coping mechanisms?

Set goals *directly related to these balancing factors* and make plans accordingly.

To see how this is done, imagine you've examined 65-year-old Mrs. Harley's balancing factors carefully and arrived at these conclusions:

• *Patient has unrealistic perception of problem.* Your nursing diagnosis? Mrs. Harley is convinced she'll never regain use of her right hand, even though it's had only minor surgery. Document this and write a mutually acceptable goal related to it. For example, "Patient will express belief she'll use her hand again." Now work out a plan, including Mrs. Harley, that'll help her achieve that goal. For a good beginning, ask: "Have you shared your concern with your doctor?"

• *Patient lacks situational supports.* Mrs. Harley has no one to turn to for emotional support during her hospitalization because she's a widow and her only daughter lives far away. Document this as your nursing diagnosis and write a goal related to it. For example: "Patient will get temporary support she needs from other sources." Now—with her assistance—work out a plan that'll help her achieve that goal. Here are some suggestions: Set times when you or another nurse can visit with her. Bring other patients to her room and encourage her to make reciprocal visits (provided it's permitted). Offer to contact her church or a friendly neighbor. Call her daughter and arrange a time when they can talk on the telephone.

• *Patient can't use her regular coping mechanisms.* As you talk to Mrs. Harley, you discover she usually copes with day-to-day stress by walking her dog through the nature preserve, doing "hand work," and working in her garden. None of these things are available to her in the hospital. What's more, she fears she'll never enjoy them again because of her surgery. Document these findings and write a goal like this: "With help, Mrs. Harley will find new ways to cope with the stress of hospitalization. She'll also express belief that she can return to her favorite coping mechanisms when she goes home from the hospital."

CRISIS INTERVENTION THROUGH OBSERVATION

Observe the patient in crisis. Most of the characteristics he exhibits are signposts you can use to get him back on the road to stability. Below are some guidelines to help you respond appropriately to his behavior.

When a patient:	*You can help by:*
Makes picky requests; Seems lonely; Is demanding.	Talking to him; Getting a volunteer to spend time with him.
Is overly considerate; Needs to do things "right"; Is ready to take the blame; Is slow and methodical.	Arranging his schedule so nothing unexpected happens; Making time allowances and not rushing him; Not demanding spontaneous decisions from him.
Exhibits marked skepticism; Is resentful, sarcastic, condescending, distrustful.	Being calm, self-assured; Not touching him; Not making promises; Making him feel accepted and secure; Speaking clearly to minimize misunderstandings.
Seems uncertain; Can't bear criticism; Can't sleep; Seems depressed and potentially suicidal.	Helping him explore feelings about himself; Not being cheerful or overly active (belittling his depression); Being calm and kind.
Is profane, domineering, restless; Is loving, blissful; Is subject to swift emotional changes; Has a short attention span.	Avoiding arguments; Not worrying about answers as much as just listening; Speaking in short, direct sentences; Staying calm, moving slowly, avoiding body contact.
Plays on your feelings; Always directs the conversation back to you.	Resisting his manipulative attempts by focusing back on him; Giving him something physical to do.

Discouraging inappropriate coping mechanisms

Every time you look in on Mr. Wilson, a recent amputee, he appears to be sleeping. After checking his medication list and his chart for other nurses' comments, you suspect he's using sleep to escape his problems. How can you help him find a more effective coping mechanism?

• First, comment on his unusual behavior. Say, "Mr. Wilson, you seem to be sleeping a lot more lately." Then give him a chance to respond. He may explain why he sleeps so much by saying, "Physical therapy tires me out," or "When I sleep, I don't think about my problems."

• Encourage him to find alternative coping mechanisms. If physical therapy tires him, suggest a nap beforehand. Involving him in occupational therapy may also discourage excessive sleeping.

• Discuss the problems he expects from his amputation. Tell him how others have coped with similar problems. To help him perceive the situation realistically, arrange a visit from someone who's coping successfully with amputation.

• Don't expect the patient to switch to a new coping mechanism with ease. Remember, as he faces his problems squarely, he'll no doubt become frustrated. Offer emotional support, no matter how long it takes him to adapt to his amputation. And continue to remind him, if necessary, sleeping won't solve his problem.

Now, discuss this with her, focusing your attention on her immediate feelings. Ask her what would make her feel better *at that moment* and try to provide it. She might suggest something as simple as a cup of tea, or a soothing back rub. (For more tips on how to help a patient find alternate coping mechanisms, read the margin on this page.)

Explore options

Remember, always include the patient when you're making plans. No matter how good your interventions look on his care plan, you won't get him to cooperate with them if he doesn't want to. When you make these decisions for your patient, you rob him of his self-esteem. Let him feel that he's still in control of the situation by exploring options with him. Encourage him to take an active role. Say: "What else can you do in this situation?"

Try to see things from his point-of-view. Ask yourself: "Who am I making these plans to help? Me or the patient?" Then give your patient a chance to suggest an alternate plan—one he can live with.

For example, suppose you feel that sitting out in the corridor in a wheelchair will help a young amputee adjust to his changed body image. However, when you suggest it to him as an option, he says he doesn't feel like facing that many strangers so soon. Instead, he'd rather start with two or three new visitors and have them come to his room.

Nursing tip: Ever have a patient who makes a minor revision in every plan you suggest? Be understanding. He may need this coping mechanism to feel in control of a frightening situation.

When you can't help

Now let's consider another difficulty you'll confront. Sooner or later, you'll meet a patient you *can't* help—or one who *refuses* your help. What then? Follow these guidelines:

• *The patient who refuses your help*: Don't take it personally. Find some other health professional he'll talk to. Or make a referral to an appropriate agency. Or come back later and try again.

• *The patient you can't help:* If you honestly feel you can't help someone—for whatever reason—admit it to yourself, the patient, and other staff members. You don't have to explain

"Sleep is one way a patient may try to escape his problems. Encourage him to find more effective coping mechanisms."

Reacting to referral: You and your patient

Sometimes the hardest part of referring a patient is telling him you're going to do it. What'll he say? How can you make it easier for him?

• If he feels rejected, tell him: "You need more support than I can give." Promise him you'll come by to visit, and do so. If that's impractical, find some other way to stay in touch.

• If he gets angry, say: "I'm trying to do what's best for you." Give him time to cool off, and continue to be reassuring.

• If he says, "What's the use?" Try to reinstill his sense of hope. Remind him of the things he holds most dear; for example, his loved ones, his religion, his profession, and possibly, his pet.

• If he says, "I couldn't have made this decision without you," remind him of his contributions to your discussions. Then encourage him to make decisions on his own.

• If he indicates he's afraid to explore his feelings with someone else, tell him, "You've taken the biggest step by talking with me." Emphasize how far he's already come.

or apologize. Just identify the fact that you can't help that particular patient and help find someone who can.

Important: When you talk to the patient about it, don't let him think it's his fault. That would be like saying "You're a hopeless case," and will only intensify his distress.

Suppose you've already started to help a patient, but now no longer feel able to. Explore your feelings. Don't ignore or deny them. Is the patient manipulating you? Are you becoming emotionally involved? Does he make you angry? Get relief. But accept responsibility for your actions. Say how you feel to the patient and what you'll do about it. For example, say "I'm getting too deeply involved in your problem to see it objectively right know. Let me get someone else to come in and care for you." *Never* imply you can no longer help a patient.

Be honest. But never let the patient feel he's to blame for your emotions. If necessary, clarify that you're upset by his actions, not with him as a *person*.

Nursing tip: Work with a team when you're trying to help patients in severe stress. Having the support and objective viewpoints of others will help you retain emotional control.

Continue your ongoing assessment

Stay flexible. Be prepared to change your assessment and your interventions, if the situation changes. Not every plan helps. You may have to take steps to refer the patient to some other health professional or an appropriate agency. Try not to feel like you've failed if this becomes necessary. As I said in the margin of this chapter, referral is a form of intervention. Just make sure the patient's immediate needs are met while he waits for help from the other source. To find out exactly when to initiate a referral, see the end of this chapter.

Evaluate your interventions

As you work with your patient, regularly evaluate your interventions to see if they're effective. Relate your evaluations to the goals you set earlier. Ask yourself:

• Does the patient feel a restored sense of balance? Does he show return of healthy functioning?

• Does he have effective coping mechanisms for other stressful situations?

Don't rush through your evaluation. Never assume a patient

is out of crisis just because he tells you he is. Continue to observe him. He may need additional support and perhaps even close supervision.

Before he leaves your care
Hopefully, your well-planned interventions have resolved your patient's crisis—or prevented one. Before he leaves your care, help him learn from the situation.

Discuss it with him. Encourage him to talk about his feelings; for example, how they've changed (if they have), and how he's dealing with them.

Help him explore the ways he coped with the crisis or stress. Point out the positive ways he dealt with it so he recognizes his strengths. Let *him* have the option of mentioning his negative methods of coping. Don't tamper with his newfound equilibrium by suddenly starting to lecture him about his mistakes or by showing previously concealed displeasure.

If he shows he wants to talk about an ineffective or destructive coping mechanism, help him. For example, suppose he says: "I guess I really acted dumb when I started yelling the other day." You might answer: "Did it make you feel better?" If he says "Not really," ask "What would have worked better?" By doing this, you've accomplished two things: helped him identify his poor coping mechanisms, and encouraged him to explore new ones.

Do everything you can to reinforce your patient's strengths and give him realistic hope for the future. Before he leaves the hospital, investigate the support systems he'll have at home. Does he have any? If not, enlist the help of family members or friends—or call the social service department. Don't let your patient go back into crisis because he lacks the support he needs. His equilibrium may still be shaky. In many cases, one crisis falls on the heels of another.

How's the rest of the family holding up? If you can, quickly assess each one's balancing factors to determine his stress level. Having someone in crisis leaves other family members and loved ones vulnerable. Be alert for increased stress and try to help.

Remember these guidelines
Now you have some idea what crisis intervention is all about. Remember the guidelines I've given you in this chapter so you

can apply them to specific patients. In subsequent sections of this book, you'll learn additional ways to deal with special problems. Take careful note of those tips. Then combine them with the general guidelines I've presented here, and work out interventions that'll help your patients. Be a nurse who knows how to prevent a crisis, as well as how to relieve one.

When to refer the patient and his family
In some crises, the best way to intervene may be to initiate a referral. Take action to refer a patient in the following situations:
• When you and other staff members can no longer deal with his behavior.
• When he doesn't respond to any of your attempts to intervene, or you're afraid that he's remaining in one stage of grief too long.
• When he seems persistently out of touch with reality, behaves bizarrely.
• When you can't strengthen or replace balancing factors.
• When you're afraid he'll attempt suicide or commit homicide.
• When you're unable to strengthen or replace balancing factors.

SKILLCHECK 1

1. Which of the following statements is false about people in crisis?
   a) A child's unlikely to experience a crisis.
   b) A person who's at a maturational point in life is especially prone to crisis.
   c) Any person can experience a crisis at any stage of life.
   d) A nurse can experience crisis, even when she's skillful at crisis intervention.
   e) A crisis is always set off by a triggering factor.

2. When in crisis, your patient may:
   a) Cope adequately with little support from you and other professionals.
   b) Be unaware of the severity of the problem or deny its existence.
   c) Try to deal with the crisis with inappropriate or harmful coping mechanisms.
   d) a and c above.
   e) All of the above.

3. When you're helping a patient in crisis, you may:
   a) Involve a family member.
   b) Involve your co-workers to insure consistent and appropriate intervention.
   c) Get an order for a tranquilizer.
   d) Contact a psychiatric nurse for help.
   e) Refer the patient to a social worker.
   f) All of the above.
   g) a, b, e above.

4. Which of the following are triggering factors for crisis?
   a) A death in the family one month earlier.
   b) A transfer to another room or unit.
   c) A postponed surgical procedure or diagnostic test.
   d) All of the above.
   e) b and c above.

5. Mrs. DeMarco has just been admitted to your floor for diagnostic tests. She knows her doctor suspects a brain tumor. By evening, she has become so upset that she cries uncontrollably and refuses dinner. Recognizing signs of crisis, you decide to intervene. You sit down with her and:
   a) Take her mind off her problems by steering the conversation away from the tests.
   b) Discuss her anxieties with her, but encourage her to do most of the talking.
   c) Discuss her anxieties with her, but help her relax by doing most of the talking yourself.
   d) Tell her all you know about the tests, including what to expect during them, so she'll be better prepared to face them.

6. Which of the following patients do you think may go into crisis?
   a) Arthur Barrow is a 69-year-old patient who recently suffered a myocardial infarction. He's been told he must adjust to a new diet and exercise schedule after he leaves the hospital. To help, his wife volunteers to go on the diet with him. She also tries to cheer him up by reminding him he'll still be able to play golf. When she leaves, Mr. Barrow tells you he doesn't think he has the energy or willpower to adjust to the changes. Do you think he faces crisis?
   b) Lorry Barnhart, a 28-year-old professional swimmer and housewife, is about to have a radical mastectomy. You're present when she cries and tells her husband she doesn't think she can face it. Although he seems very unsettled, he reassures her the surgery won't affect how he feels towards her. Do you think she faces crisis?
   c) Fourteen-year-old Mark Thomas' father is dying of cancer. When you're caring for Mr. Thomas, he confides that he hasn't told Mark how seriously ill he is. But he figures that isn't necessary. He says, "Mark's a smart boy. He probably knows I'm dying." Mark continues to visit his father after school for several weeks. One day on his way out, he asks you when his father's going to be discharged. Do you think Mark faces possible crisis?

(Answers on page 179)

HELPING
THE PATIENT
AND HIS FAMILY
IN CRISIS

"Unpredictable changes and constant variations in day-to-day care upset a stressed patient and may throw him into panic."

"Respect your patient's limitations. Don't expect too much from him, especially on days when his routine has been upset."

"The trouble with denial and other psychologic defenses is, they interfere with your perception. When this happens, you leave your crisis patient without the support he needs to restore his equilibrium."

"You may see an occasional patient who hides extreme stress under an unusually calm, composed exterior. Try to estimate his internal stress level. It may be greater than that of the patient who shows his distress."

"Whatever you do, never give a patient or his family the impression that you're criticizing them, trying to impart your own values, or acting as their judge."

3

Helping the patient overcome a distorted body image

BY THERESA CROUSHORE, RN

YOU'RE WORKING on the medical-surgical floor of an upstate hospital, caring for Gary Hudson, a star football player from a nearby university. Two days earlier, Gary's left arm was badly mutilated in a boating accident. Because the arm was irreparably damaged, doctors amputated it just below the shoulder.

Now, as you approach Gary to check his dressing, he asks you to hold his hands. "Not just that hand," he says, when you reach out. "Hold both of them."

Slightly startled, you hesitate. Does he really see his missing left arm, unable to imagine himself without it? Has the accident thrown him into crisis? How can you intervene to help him?

"Gary, I'm holding your right hand," you say gently. "Your left hand and arm were amputated the day of the boating accident."

Like many patients who—through accident or surgery—suddenly must adjust to a radically altered body image, Gary's going to need a lot of help.

In this chapter, I'll teach you how to give that help. First, I'll explain how a patient's body image—or his perception of himself—can affect his recovery from illness or surgery. Then

I'll teach you how to apply what you've learned to patient care. Among other things, you'll discover practical ways to:
- define body image
- spot unusual behavior that may indicate when a patient's body image is threatened
- recognize common triggering events that may propel such a patient into crisis
- assess his balancing factors
- strengthen those factors to prevent crises.

What is body image, anyway?
As you probably know, the term *body image* means more than just what we think about our appearance. It also includes how we perceive such things as our own intelligence, our sexuality, and our physical strength and endurance. Along with our values, beliefs, personal goals, and other people's opinions of us, the way we perceive ourselves physically shapes how we feel about ourselves as persons.

We start life with no body image at all. During infancy, we gradually learn to distinguish between self and surroundings. We become aware that we're separate from our parents. Then, we begin to gain control over our bodily functions. Throughout the rapid growth of childhood and adolescence, our body image and the way we feel about ourselves as persons continues to change. By the time we're adults, what we think of ourselves has become so intimately associated with our body image that any threat to that image is very frightening.

In fact, any change in function or appearance of a body part can threaten body image. For this to happen, the change needn't be as drastic as the loss of a limb. It may be something like loss of sexual drive, or a sudden fluctuation in weight. Any of these can be almost as psychologically devastating as the threat of imminent death.

Remember, no two people see themselves in exactly the same way. What seriously affects one person's body image may scarcely affect another's. For example, a patient may feel her body image so threatened by having a nasogastric tube that she refuses all visitors.

Common sense suggests that body image ends where the body itself ends. Yet these boundaries may vary, depending on the patient's individual perception. Hair, nails, and even clothing are also part of body image, though they're not equally

"An adult's self-image is so intimately associated with his physical being. Any change in his body image can be a frightening and traumatic experience."

After the amputation: The phantom limb

If your patient's had a limb amputated recently, he may be troubled by the eerie sensation that it's still attached to him. He may even complain that he feels pain or itching in the missing arm or leg.

Don't assume this indicates he's using denial to cope with his change in body image. The truth is this: Phantom limb phenomenon has a simple physiologic explanation. Newly severed nerve endings continue to send impulses that mimic messages from the missing limb. Until these nerves heal, the patient will experience confusing sensations. Rationally, he knows the limb's gone, but his nervous system tells him it's still there.

Help him get through this difficult period by reassuring him and his family that he's not crazy, but that what he's feeling is a normal aftereffect of his amputation. Tell them that the disturbing sensations will go away, probably within 6 weeks.

What else can you do? Avoid irritating the amputation site unnecessarily. Keep it padded and tightly wrapped.

important to everyone. For instance, some people think nothing of biting their nails short, whereas others become upset when they break a long fingernail. Body image also includes objects that are always with us, like a watch or a wedding ring. Losing such an object can cause stress, which may lead to crisis if the loss is regretted.

Let me give you an example: Imagine you're caring for 63-year-old Tony Vernon, who'll be having surgery to repair an inguinal hernia. In preparation, you ask him to remove his eyeglasses, jewelry, and clothes. Then after he's seated on the bed in a hospital gown, you ask him to remove his dentures. Anxiously, he looks around the room. Then, he says firmly, "No way. Do what you like, but my dentures stay in." Mr. Vernon, like all of us, fears a loss of image. And you're taking away all the props he needs to support it. What can you do?

First, recognize when your patient's telling you he's concerned about his body image. Obviously, you can't let Mr. Vernon keep his dentures in during surgery if you've been ordered not to. However, tell him you understand his concern. Explain why his dentures can't stay in and assure him they'll be returned before he has visitors.

Watch for signals

Of course, the patient who's expressing concern about his body image isn't necessarily in crisis. How, then, can you tell if he is? Use the assessment skills you learned in the previous chapters.

Watch for unusual behavior that may indicate a threatened body image. For example, ask yourself:

• *Does the patient act rebellious?* Mr. Vernon's protest clearly indicated he perceived a threat to his body image.

• *Does the patient show anger and hostility?* The patient who lashes out is trying, unsuccessfully, to cope with overwhelming stress. Don't take it personally; look for the true source of his anger. You may find it's related to a threatened body image.

• *Does the patient refuse to socialize?* Fearing rejection, the patient concerned with body image may shun others, including family and friends. Don't assume this fear is groundless. Some families can't accept a patient as he is after a disfiguring accident or surgery. Their shock automatically eliminates them as available support systems.

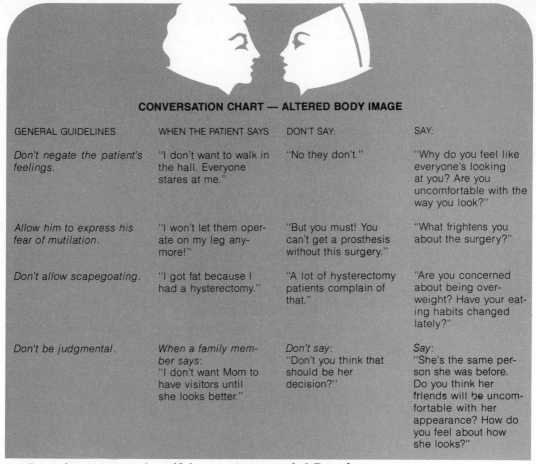

CONVERSATION CHART — ALTERED BODY IMAGE

GENERAL GUIDELINES	WHEN THE PATIENT SAYS	DON'T SAY:	SAY:
Don't negate the patient's feelings.	"I don't want to walk in the hall. Everyone stares at me."	"No they don't."	"Why do you feel like everyone's looking at you? Are you uncomfortable with the way you look?"
Allow him to express his fear of mutilation.	"I won't let them operate on my leg anymore!"	"But you must! You can't get a prosthesis without this surgery."	"What frightens you about the surgery?"
Don't allow scapegoating.	"I got fat because I had a hysterectomy."	"A lot of hysterectomy patients complain of that."	"Are you concerned about being overweight? Have your eating habits changed lately?"
Don't be judgmental.	When a family member says: "I don't want Mom to have visitors until she looks better."	Don't say: "Don't you think that should be her decision?"	Say: "She's the same person she was before. Do you think her friends will be uncomfortable with her appearance? How do you feel about how she looks?"

• *Does the patient make self-deprecating remarks?* Does he say, "I never was very attractive anyway." Maybe he's looking for a compliment, some reassurance that he's okay despite a changed appearance.

• *Does the patient avoid looking at or touching an altered body part, such as a stoma?* Chances are, he's trying to cope by dissociating himself from the changed body image. If so, his equilibrium's in danger.

• *Does the patient refer to a missing part as if it were present?* Such distorted perceptions may well indicate he's using denial to cope with the change.

• *Does the patient refuse to participate in his care?* The patient who shows no interest in personal hygiene or reason-

HOW TO HELP THE DYING PATIENT

"It isn't death I'm afraid of so much. It's dying," a cancer patient told his nurse. Does that surprise you? It shouldn't. In most cases, a dying patient's greatest concerns are how he'll face death and how his family will manage afterwards.

Do all you can to help him. Begin by accepting his attitude no matter what stage of grief he's in. Then follow these stress-relieving guidelines:

• *Allay his fears.* A dying patient's fears usually encompass three levels: fear of pain, fear of loneliness, and fear of meaninglessness. Of the three, fear of pain is probably the most acute and realistic. To allay this fear, constantly reassure the patient that he'll be kept comfortable with medication and that you won't forget him.

What about loneliness? Most nurses who have cared for dying patients say this: When the patient's by himself, his pain always seems worse than when he has someone to comfort him. He doesn't want to die alone. Having you or his loved ones near by may be all he really needs to feel he's not abandoned.

Fear that his life has been meaningless is probably the most devastating fear of a dying patient. Chances are, no matter how successful he's been—or how well-liked—he'll review parts of his life with regret and despair over his failures. Try to listen understandingly. Give him a chance to talk. Then, when he mentions a positive contribution he's made to life, encourage him to tell you more. Reinforce his good feelings about that part of his life by asking about it from time to time. Tell his loved ones how he

feels and urge them to do the same.

• *Give him control.* Let the dying patient make decisions whenever possible. Don't decide what you think he needs. For example, suppose he doesn't want to see visitors one day. Respect his wish, whether you think he needs company or not. Explain to visitors that he wants time to himself. By allowing the dying patient to control his last days, you permit him to die with dignity. Make this consideration primary in your care.

• *Encourage him to set new goals.* Don't worry that he'll attempt something unrealistic. Chances are, he'll concentrate only on problems he can solve.

For example, he may want to complete a project he started before he became ill. Try to arrange any scheduled treatments so he has time to work on it.

• *Talk with him.* He may want to reminisce about things that are meaningful to him. For example when you check him at bedtime, he may say, "When I was a little boy, my mother used to tell me a story before I went to sleep." Spend a few moments talking to him about this, if you can. Sharing a pleasant memory may help comfort him.

He may also need someone he can talk to about death. The patient may feel that talking about his impending death with his family will upset them. Listen understandingly. Help him sort out his feelings by showing him that you accept him as he is.

• *Level with him.* Be honest with the dying patient. When he asks for information about his

condition, try to supply it. But accept your own limitations. If he asks or says something that makes you uncomfortable, say so. If you can't deal with it, get another nurse to help. Your candor will strengthen your rapport.

Don't forget, he wants honest answers about his family's welfare, too. He cares as deeply for them when he's dying as he did when he was well. Reassure him as much as you can. Don't permit worry about loved ones to increase his pain and stress level.

• *Make him secure.* Surround the dying patient with familiar objects. If he wants a picture, book, or blanket from home, encourage the family to bring it. Sometimes small requests are the most important. Consider Mrs. Wagner, who's dying from cancer. More than anything else, she wants to see her grandchild. Ask someone to bring the child to the hospital.

• *Involve the family.* Give the family a chance to do something tangible to help their loved one. For example, just sitting at the bedside might make them feel frustrated and helpless. Because quality physical care means so much to most families, involve them in it. Let them help reposition the patient. Teach them to care for his back and skin.

Reassure the family that you and the rest of the staff will do everything possible to relieve the patient's pain. Encourage them to speak freely about the patient's impending death. In the words of one nurse, death can be life's last great experience. We can learn great lessons in courage from the terminally ill.

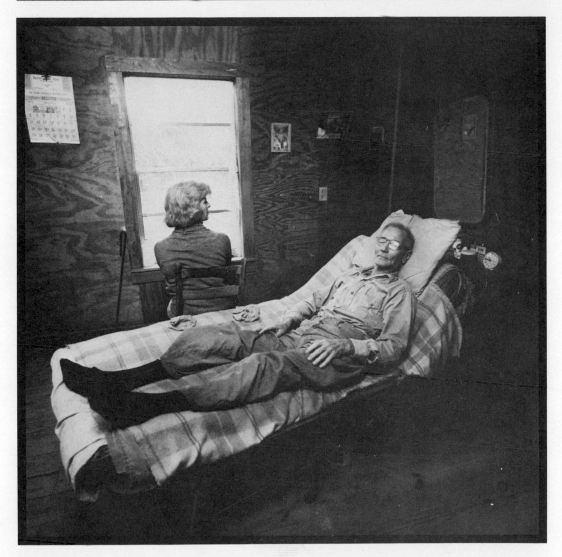

"In many cases, the dying patient copes with death by isolating himself from family and friends. The people around him misinterpret what he's doing and resent it."

able exercise may be rejecting an altered body image.

Does your patient's behavior suggest he's in severe stress because of a threatened body image? Continue your assessment. Be sure to document what you observe. In this way, you'll alert other staff members to a potential crisis.

Looking for a triggering event
Watch for things that may threaten a patient's body image. Common triggering events include:
- *surgery.* Even minor surgery violates the body's integrity.
- *change in function or capability.* A cerebrovascular accident, an acute arthritis attack, or even a new prosthesis such as a hearing aid may trigger a body-image crisis.
- *hormonal imbalance.* Besides occurring during puberty, pregnancy, and menopause, hormonal imbalance may stem from medication or surgical alterations. For instance, a male patient whose treatment plan includes estrogen therapy may feel threatened knowing he's receiving a "female hormone."
- *traumatic injury.* Any injury, even one that doesn't interfere much with function or mobility, may trigger a body-image disturbance.

If any of these events has occurred to the patient during the last few weeks, he's probably under considerable stress. If it's severe enough, his coping energies can quickly become exhausted. But will he go into crisis? He may if two or more of his balancing factors are weak or missing. What can you do to prevent a crisis?

Before I explain how, let me remind you that sometimes swift action is necessary. In certain cases, your judgment may suggest an immediate intervention before you've finished a complete assessment of your patient's balancing factors. But for clarity's sake, I'll tell you what steps you'd go through to make a thorough assessment.

Assess your patient's balancing factors
Suppose you're caring for 38-year-old Mrs. Carson, whose left eye was removed 2 days ago after a traumatic injury. Realizing that such an event places tremendous stress on her body image, you begin assessing her balancing factors:
- *How does she perceive her altered body image?* Does she continually touch her dressing? Does she use her right eye, or keep it closed? Is she preoccupied with another injury that's comparatively minor?

BODY-IMAGE CRISIS: GUIDELINES FOR INTERVENTION

Adjusting to a sudden change in body image is stressful, even for the strongest-willed patient. Here are some specific examples of cases where your knowledge of crisis intervention can help you care effectively for the patient with a threatened body image:

Case 1

Fifteen-year-old Don James was hospitalized for severe burns over his entire back. He'd been camping when the tent he was sleeping in caught fire. Don barely managed to escape. A nurse asked him the inevitable question: "How were you burned?" "I burned myself by being stupid," Don replied. "Does that make you happy?"

Suppose you were that nurse. With a thoughtful response, you may be able to ease Don's bitterness and help him face his condition more positively. How?

Others eventually will ask him about his accident, so don't avoid the question. Recognize his angry reply is a form of release, and accept it as such. Be supportive. Say, "It must be hard for you to think about. Would you like to talk about it?"

Be realistic with him. While he's in your care, prepare him to deal with his altered self-image by talking about his condition in a gentle, straight-forward way.

When you care for a burn patient, also keep in mind:
• If you need to wear gloves in caring for his burns, explain why. Don't let him think he's repulsive to touch.
• If the patient's in isolation, talk to him from the door before you put on your mask and gown. Don't neglect the isolated patient; stop in regularly, even if putting on special clothing's inconvenient.
• If a patient's face is burned, don't avoid looking at his face and eyes when you communicate. By the same token, don't stare; you'll make him feel uneasy.
• Remember, some eschar is removed each time the patient goes to physical therapy for whirlpool treatments. This may so disturb the patient that he perceives the treatments as further assaults on his already threatened body image. Be understanding.

Case 2

Mrs. Jennings, a 42-year-old lawyer, was hospitalized for throat surgery. After the operation, she couldn't speak for several weeks. During her recovery, health-team members felt embarrassed after making comments like "Did you call for me?" or "Did you talk to your son today?" Mrs. Jennings already felt uneasy about her condition; sensing others' embarrassment made her feel worse.

Now let's put you in this situation. By thinking positively, you can turn a potentially embarrassing statement into a beneficial one for both you and the patient. How?

First, remember that awkward statements aren't always taken literally. Be yourself. Second, don't be so afraid of saying the wrong thing that you say nothing. Usually, even if you do say something inappropriate, the patient'll appreciate your thoughtfulness—if he senses you're genuinely concerned about him. What if Mrs. Jennings does pick up on your statement? Use the opportunity for patient teaching. Correcting unrealistic perceptions will help her accept her altered body image.

Case 3

Twenty-eight-year-old Mrs. White gave birth to a 6-pound boy. Two days later, she was ready to go home. But when her pre-pregnancy clothes didn't fit, she broke down in tears. "You just have postpartum blues," a nurse told her offhandedly, and let her go.

Now let's put you in this picture. By asking a few simple questions, you could help Mrs. White understand and adjust to her new body image. And you could determine if something besides her changed appearance has upset her. How?

Take time to sit down and talk with Mrs. White so she understands that you care. Find out why she's crying. Say "You seem upset. What's bothering you?" If she's disturbed by her new appearance—flabby abdomen, swollen breasts, an episiotomy—assure her that her condition's normal and transient. Explain, for instance, that her uterus will return to its usual size in about 3 months, with proper diet and exercise.

Don't assume her crying stems solely from her appearance. Something else may be upsetting her. Help her express her other feelings:
• Find out if her perception of motherhood is realistic. Sometimes a changed personal appearance causes resentment of the child, leading possibly to child abuse.
• Ask if she has adequate support from her husband. If not, seek a relative, a neighbor, or close friend to be with her temporarily.
• Remember your limitations. After asking questions and talking with the mother, refer her to other help, if necessary.

THE PATIENT'S FAMILY: AN IMPORTANT BALANCING FACTOR

For the patient who's facing a change in body image, the chief source of emotional support is usually his family. Without that support, he's missing an important balancing factor that he needs to keep him out of crisis. Find out if he's got that support.

Talk with family members to determine how they perceive your patient's changed body image. Their reactions will affect how successfully he adapts to the change. For instance, if they perceive his amputation as grotesque, their attitude will communicate itself and undermine his self-acceptance.

Before family members visit him, talk to them to learn what they expect to find: "Tell me what you've been told about Linda's condition." "Have you ever seen someone on a respirator?" If the change is drastic, try to lessen the shock for them. Be sure to explain any machines, tubing, and traction devices so they won't be frightened by them. Assure them that their loved one is still the same person he was before the change.

Further tips:
• Be alert to family members' verbal and nonverbal behavior. For instance, silence or hesitation may signal an unwillingness to be supportive. But don't automatically exclude family members who seem initially hesitant to take an active role.
• Tell the family how the patient feels in general terms. Don't focus, for instance, on his amputation or his traction. Say "Gary's comfortable, enjoying a TV show right now." Or, "Gary's worried about how he looks right now."
• Point out the patient's restrictions and abilities. "Gary needs to have someone with him, but he can get around well with some help."
• Encourage touching. Say "Gary's more comfortable with someone beside him when he walks. Without his arm, he's still a little unsteady."

With the family and patient, formulate a plan to achieve concrete and realistic objectives. For instance, determine that after 3 days, Gary will dress himself in 10 minutes with one arm.
• Seek support of family members to implement the plan. Say "I'm concerned about Gary and believe you can help." Explain your concern and list your expectations. Say for instance, "I think Gary would do better if you were here more often."
• Relate the plan to the patient's level of dependence: The less able the patient, the more active you and the family need to be.
• Respect patient and family's culture and beliefs: Don't impose your value system on them.
• Be available during visits. Tell the family where you'll be for advice and when you'll be there. Then be punctual.

• *How is she trying to cope with the stress?* Is she refusing to see visitors? Is she insisting the room be kept dark? Does she look away when you're talking with her?

• *Are her support systems available?* Is she a local resident? Was her husband involved in the accident? Can she call on relatives or friends in the area for emotional support?

Strengthen those balancing factors

As you recall, unless two or more balancing factors are present, your patient needs immediate help to avert a crisis. Let's examine how you can apply what you've learned in Chapter 2 to help Mrs. Carson effectively.

As you continue your assessment, you notice that she avoids looking at you and other staff members. Tell her what you've observed. Encourage her to discuss her feelings but watch for the nonverbal responses, too: For example, does she clench her hands or assume a defensive posture? By allowing her to express how she feels about the loss of her eye, you begin to understand how it's affected her body image. How does she perceive it? "I know how horrible I must look" she says. "I just can't stand the thought of people staring at me." When you ask her why she thinks they will, you find out she has the mistaken notion that she'll have to wear an ugly patch over her eye. Obviously, she has a completely unrealistic perception of her body image. Take steps to correct that perception. With proper patient teaching, you can alleviate some of her anxiety. Explain that, in 3 to 6 weeks, she'll get an artificial eye that'll look amazingly normal.

Meanwhile, try to prepare her to deal with other people's perceptions of her. Whether she's ready or not, there'll be people who'll ask about her eye, so don't deny this. Encourage her to talk to other patients. Visit her as much as possible, and encourage other staff members to do the same.

Be sure she understands realistically how the change will affect her lifestyle. For example, she'll need to adapt her driving habits to compensate for impaired peripheral vision and depth perception. By talking with her about her activities and future plans, you're not only identifying any new limitations and restrictions, but helping her to accept them.

How is she attempting to cope with her stress? Does she refuse to see visitors? Such action may ease her stress temporarily, but it won't solve her long-term problem. Do your best to help her find a more effective coping mechanism, so she can maintain her equilibrium.

Begin by asking her how she usually copes with stress. Then look for ways she can use her regular coping mechanisms in her new situation. If some of these coping mechanisms seem impractical in a hospital setting, help her to find alternate coping mechanisms as a temporary substitute. *Nursing tip:* Supply combs, brushes, and other grooming aids to encourage your patient to get involved with her new body image. In most hospitals, you can obtain a personal care kit from central supply. Or, better still, ask the patient's family to bring in some of her own things.

Are her support systems working? As you talk to Mrs. Carson, you learn that her husband is away on a business trip. Soon after he's contacted, he arrives at the hospital. When you tell him about his wife's condition, you're relieved by his obvious concern. He's already thinking about ways to comfort

The amputated limb: What to say about it

If your patient's about to have a limb amputated, he may ask you how the hospital plans to dispose of it.

Take his concern seriously. Remember, some religions have strict codes governing disposal of body parts. No matter how you feel, respect your patient's wishes and help him make the arrangements he wants. For example, he may ask you to contact a funeral director to assure a proper burial for an amputated arm.

In any case, know how your hospital usually disposes of body parts so you can tell any patient who asks. Never act surprised or make him feel uncomfortable about asking. Remember, his interest is perfectly normal.

ADJUSTING TO LIFE-SUSTAINING EQUIPMENT

Only a few days ago, Mrs. Sims was a housewife leading a normal life. Now, after a car accident, she's at the mercy of a noisy, impersonal contraption looming at her bedside. As much as she resents it, she knows the respirator's keeping her alive.

Living with a respirator
Total dependence on a machine like a respirator can threaten a patient's body image as severely as an amputation or a colostomy. Assess and strengthen her balancing factors as you would for any patient with an altered body image. You can support her further if you:
• Communicate with her as normally as possible. Don't stop talking to her just because she can't talk back—you'll just increase her sense of isolation and hopelessness. Instead, devise a system that allows her to respond to you in some way. If she can write, a pad and pencil may be all you need.

Be imaginative. If she can move only her eyelids easily, work out a yes-no system using blinks. Become sensitive to hand signals, facial expressions, and body language. Repeat what you think she said and wait for a yes or no from her. Be sure to share the signals you've worked out with other team members.
• Explain how the machine works and prepare her for anything unusual. For example, tell her when you're going to change the depth of her respirations and why you're doing it. Otherwise, the sudden deep breaths are likely to scare her.

Explain the machine's alarm system and what might set it off. Gain her confidence by re-

sponding promptly to alarms.
• Insist on normal attention to hygiene. If the patient's physically able, encourage her to take part in a personal hygiene program. Anything that restores some control over her body will strengthen her sense of dignity and self-worth.
• Remember that Mrs. Sims, not the machine, is the patient. When you enter her room, focus your attention first on her, not the respirator.

Leaving the respirator
Eventually Mrs. Sims recovers enough to be weaned from the respirator. But when you tell her the news, she becomes angry and resentful.

Don't be surprised by this reaction. while dependent on the respirator, she extended her body's boundaries to include the machine. Leaving it requires another traumatic adjustment.

To make her initial sessions off the respirator easier:
• Eliminate distractions. She'll have enough to do just breathing, without eating or entertaining visitors at the same time.
• Answer her call light immediately. If she's not sure you'll respond promptly to her call, she may refuse to go off the respirator the next time.
• Keep sessions brief. Gradually extend them as her confidence grows.

When the patient's a child
Suppose you're caring for a child who's on a respirator? Chances are, he'll need your special consideration. Why? Because being separated from his parents will no doubt frighten him. He'll also feel upset because he can't move around

freely. Here's how to help:
• Explain simply how the respirator works, and what noises he can expect to hear. This may help him relax, so he doesn't fight it.
• Give him as much room to move about as possible. If the doctor says it's O.K., use a jacket restraint. Doing so will allow you to free his hands, but still immobilize his torso. As a precaution have him wear mittens. Make puppet faces on the mittens so he can entertain himself.
• Make sure you secure his endotracheal or tracheostomy tube well.
• Reassure him that his parents haven't deserted him. If possible, arrange it so one or both of them can hold or rock him.
• Provide him with ways to entertain himself. If his hands are free, he probably can play some simple games with a parent or volunteer.

What about the respirator patient who's suffered brain death?
Should mechanical, life-sustaining treatment be continued? Obviously, only the family and doctor can decide. Extend emotional support to family members, but —
• Don't tell them what to do. If they ask for your opinion, tell them you can't help them decide. Beware of influencing them with a careless remark about the patient's prognosis.
• Don't change your attitude toward the family after the decision's made. Continue to support them, but avoid expressing your opinion of their choice.
• Don't change the care you give the patient during or after the decision-making process.

"Imagine how terrified a child feels when he's on a respirator. Not only is he separated from his parents, but he's lost his normal ability to communicate."

and reassure her. Help him understand the stress his wife is experiencing by explaining her fears of rejection. Encourage him to respond.

Remember, having someone in crisis leaves other family members vulnerable. Evaluate Mr. Carson's stress level, and help him find other sources of emotional support for his wife and himself.

Be available during visits to answer any questions they may have. If Mr. Carson privately expresses his concern about the possibility of future surgery, make sure to include Mrs. Carson in the discussion. Even if she's not feeling up to actively participating, she'll benefit from sharing the information and seeing further evidence of her husband's concern. (For more information on how to help families of patients in crisis, see page 52.)

Some last words

Of course, no two patients have exactly the same problem, or the same perception of that problem. Because of this, I've included some specific cases, along with appropriate interventions on page 51.

Keep in mind that anyone whose body image is threatened truly needs your support and understanding. With imagination and ingenuity, you can help your patient cope with the stress of a changed body image. If you've read this chapter carefully, you've seen how you can avert crisis by replacing a missing balancing factor or strengthening a weak one.

Where to refer the patient and his family

Give a list of the following organizations to the patient coping with a distorted body image. Include his family. To insure they get the needed information, write to these organizations yourself and keep their literature handy:

● American Foundation for the Blind, 15 W. 16th Street, New York, N.Y. 10011

● National Association for the Deaf, 814 Thayer Avenue, Silver Spring, Md. 20910

● National Association of the Physically Handicapped, 76 Elm Street, London, Ohio 43140

● Association of Rehabilitation Facilities, 5530 Wisconsin Avenue NW, Washington, D.C. 20015.

4

Supporting survivors of unexpected death

BY PATRICIA SUE SHARER, RN

WHEN A SERIOUSLY INJURED accident victim is brought into the emergency department, or a patient who'd been doing well suddenly takes a turn for the worse, your first concern, of course, is saving that patient's life. You pour all your energy into lifesaving tasks. You don't always have time to think about the family—to find out how they're coping with the extreme stress.

But suppose the patient dies despite your efforts. Even though you're emotionally exhausted, the survivors need your help now. How can you help survivors who've had little or no preparation for death? What can you do for the family of a patient you didn't even know?

No one can predict how people will react to a family member's sudden death. But an understanding of the grieving process can help you deal with a wide variety of reactions. Remember what you learned in Chapters 1 and 2 about balancing factors. With adequate support systems, people in grief will exercise various coping mechanisms to accept death's reality. To make the survivor's grieving as easy as possible, try to minimize his extreme stress. That will help him maintain his equilibrium.

YOUR GRIEVING PROCESS

You go through a grieving process every time one of your patients dies. What are the stages? How do you react to them? Here are some sample behaviors:

When you:	And justify it by saying:	You may be in this stage:
Are *overly* efficient and don't talk to survivors except to give routine information	"I've got too much to do. Besides, if they needed help they'd ask for it."	Denial, avoidance
Lash out at co-workers	"Why didn't somebody reorder drugs the last time there was a Code? Wouldn't it be nice to have a stocked unit in an emergency?"	Anger
Go about your tasks subdued, sullenly	"It was probably my fault. I still can't deal with emergencies."	Depression
Are *overly* concerned with details when you deal with patients and their families	"If I do everything perfect, no one else in my care will die."	Rationalization
Show compassion to patients and their families; can discuss death; show your emotions	"I'm here to help."	Acceptance

Remember: Normal functions are not necessarily impaired by grief. But you must pass through the above stages when your patient dies, or after his death. If you linger in any intermediate stage, you may upset your equilibrium. Talk to another nurse or an understanding friend. Prolonged grieving for one patient may keep you from helping others.

Stages of grief

As you know, grief has definite, predictable stages. The first stage is usually shock or denial. In it, the survivor may seem numb, as if he's in a daze. This reaction is one way of coping with intense, overwhelming pain.

During this stage, don't expect the survivor to make decisions. When you gather routine information in the E.D. about the victim, take your time. Let the survivor talk to you, if he wants, about his lost loved one. Give him something to do, so he'll have an outlet that will help relieve his feelings of helplessness. Let him know you understand he's under great stress. When words fail, touching can be an effective way of saying that you care. In many cases, your presence itself may be a comfort.

The survivor may move into the second stage of grieving within moments, or avoid it for as long as 2 weeks. As he gains a realistic perception of the situation, he may develop strong feelings of anguish, helplessness, and frustration. Is he on the verge of tears? He may feel uncomfortable crying in front of strangers. Say, "It's okay to cry." Then give him privacy, if

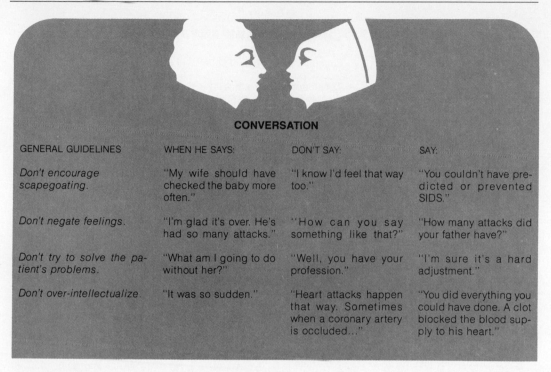

CONVERSATION

GENERAL GUIDELINES	WHEN HE SAYS:	DON'T SAY:	SAY:
Don't encourage scapegoating.	"My wife should have checked the baby more often."	"I know I'd feel that way too."	"You couldn't have predicted or prevented SIDS."
Don't negate feelings.	"I'm glad it's over. He's had so many attacks."	"How can you say something like that?"	"How many attacks did your father have?"
Don't try to solve the patient's problems.	"What am I going to do without her?"	"Well, you have your profession."	"I'm sure it's a hard adjustment."
Don't over-intellectualize.	"It was so sudden."	"Heart attacks happen that way. Sometimes when a coronary artery is occluded..."	"You did everything you could have done. A clot blocked the blood supply to his heart."

you think it'll make him more comfortable.

Some survivors show signs of emotional and somatic distress: chest pain, weakness, sighing, or fainting. Occasionally, these disorders are caused by conflicting emotions. For example, consider the survivor who wasn't at the hospital when his loved one died. If he blames himself for this, guilt may be intensifying his anguish. *Caution:* Don't blindly assume a survivor's disorders are caused by grief. He may be having a heart attack or stroke and need immediate medical attention.

In the second stage, the survivor may lash out in anger. For example, suppose he makes unfounded accusations about you and the hospital? Try not to be defensive. In most cases, he's venting his stress. Instead, help him by saying calmly, "You're understandably upset. It's hard when someone you love dies."

Later, a survivor may go through other grief stages: rationalization, depression, identification, and seclusion. (However, you probably won't see many of these in the hospital.) Hopefully, he'll then progress to the last stage: accepting his loss. But he can't be hurried. Grieving, like wound healing, takes time.

WHEN THE BABY DIES: HOW YOU CAN HELP THE FAMILY

When a woman's had a spontaneous abortion or stillbirth, she and her husband need your special attention. To help in either case, follow all the suggestions outlined in the main portion of this chapter and add these considerations:

• Don't make careless or judgmental statements. For example, never say: "You can always have another baby" or "It's all for the best." Instead, say: "It must be hard to lose something you've planned on." Don't encourage "replacing" the child with another.

Give them a chance to ask questions and express their emotions. Remember, their grief has just begun; they'll need time to get over the initial shock of their baby's death. What's more, they face the added burden of explaining to others how and why they lost the baby.

• Is the mother in a maternity ward? Ask her if she'd prefer to transfer to another unit. She may feel more comfortable away from the nursery.

If she prefers to stay on the ward, watch her reactions when other mothers hold their infants. Comment on your observations. Allow her this time to openly express her grief.

• Bend visiting hours. Let the husband stay with his wife as long as possible, to make grieving easier. His support helps bolster her damaged self-image. Continue to give proper physical care. Show your support by keeping the mother clean and comfortable.

• Know where to refer the parents for possible genetic counseling. .

• Check the mother's blood type. If she's Rh negative, she'll need Rhogam.

Specific tips in case of spontaneous abortion:

• Consider the mother's level of understanding. If you think the words "spontaneous abortion" will sound bad to her, use the term "miscarriage."

• Does your state require a "Release of Responsibility for Abortion" form? Tell the parents: "You must sign this form to show the abortion was spontaneous. You also need it for insurance coverage."

• Be prepared to answer any questions she asks. For example; "What will you do with the baby now?" Tell her about the pathology identification process. If she asks what the baby's sex is, tell her if you know.

• Before the mother leaves the hospital, instruct her to call the doctor immediately in case of prolonged or excessive vaginal bleeding. Tell her when to see her doctor for a checkup.

Specific tips in case of stillbirth:

• Be honest. When a woman's had a stillborn baby, she probably senses something's wrong. Suppose the mother asks you directly: "What's wrong?" Tell her the facts: "There's a problem with the baby. But let me have the doctor give you the specific details."

• Don't refer to a stillborn baby as "it." Use the name the parents selected, or say "he" or "she."

• If the mother's heavily sedated, she may be in no condition to see her baby. So record what he looked like, including size, color of eyes, and hair. Later on, she may want to know these things. In some cases, you may want to take the baby's picture.

• Don't encourage the parents

to minimize the event. If it seems helpful, ask them if they'd like to hold the baby. They may be reluctant to ask, fearing you'll think they're morbid. If they answer yes, gently clean the baby. Be careful of delicate skin. Dress him and place him in a blanket or crib. Prepare the parents so they won't be shocked by his coloring and limpness.

• Don't bring them the baby and disappear. Stay with them awhile. Then ask if they'd like some privacy.

• If the parents decide to have a funeral service for the baby, make sure the mother's discharged to attend, even if she has to return to the hospital.

• Leaving the hospital without a baby creates an empty feeling for the couple. Gently encourage them to talk about it. "What will you do when you go home?" A big concern is what to tell friends. Ask them "What would you like them to know about it?"

How to baptize a baby

If an infant's stillborn or unlikely to survive, should you baptize him? Yes. You may also baptize an aborted fetus. Any person can perform a baptism regardless of personal religious views. Some hospitals keep a baptismal tray in the emergency room, delivery room, or nursery. If necessary, however, you can perform the sacrament with tap water. Sprinkle the water over the infant's head while saying: "I baptize thee in the name of the Father, Son, and Holy Ghost." This sacrament is mandatory in the Roman Catholic religion and, in some cases, for Episcopalian infants. For further information on religious beliefs, see pages 64 and 65.

"Few experiences are as emotionally shattering as having a still-born baby. Give the distressed family your special attention."

CRIB DEATH: THE TRAGEDY OF SIDS

When sudden infant death syndrome (SIDS) strikes, the *survivors* become your patients. How can you effectively ease their stress? What steps can you take to prevent crisis? To begin, consider the needs of each survivor and tailor your interventions to meet them.

Here are some guidelines for:

Breaking the news. The doctor should tell the entire family—at one time—about the baby's death. Encourage the parents to let any brothers or sisters sit in. The children should understand their parents had no control over the baby's death. They may believe their parents took the baby away and will do the same to them.

Confirming the death. At first many parents have trouble accepting their baby's death. So, over and over, they'll recite how they found the baby, what they did, and who they called. They're not necessarily seeking your approval. Don't just tell them, "You did the right thing." Instead, help them reconstruct the event by encouraging their recital. Ask them, "What then?" "Who was there then?" "What were you feeling?"

Invite the family to see and hold the dead baby. But first, tell the parents what to expect: facial color, temperature, body limpness. If possible, get permission to remove any I.V. lines. Then clean and dress the baby and wrap him in a blanket so his limbs don't hang lifelessly at his sides. After you bring them the baby, remain in the room. Encourage them to talk about their feelings.

Easing the guilt. When the parents don't know about SIDS, their stress and grief may be compounded by guilt. They also

face the added burden of explaining the death to family and friends. Tell them about SIDS by relaying the information we've included here. Assure them that they couldn't have anticipated or prevented their baby's death.

Dealing with autopsy. Many parents feel an autopsy is unnecessary. They say: "Our baby is dead. Does it matter why?" Tell them it does. Approximately 85% of all sudden infant deaths are unexplained. In other words, about 10,000 babies die each year in the United States alone and no one knows why. Only research can find the answer. (The remaining 15% of sudden infant deaths are explainable. They're caused by undetected accidents, child abuse, or unsuspected congenital abnormalities.)

Preventing future crises. Remember, sudden infant death can radically upset the survivors' home life, good health, and mental stability. Here are some tips you can use to ease the pain:

• Be patient with parents who delay their departure by asking one question after another. Chances are, they're reluctant to leave their dead baby.
• Give the parents SIDS information to take home with them. Then when relatives and friends ask questions, they'll have something concrete to refer to.
• Don't discourage parents who call you later to ask health advice about their other children. They're probably seeking reassurance that they're doing things right.
• Be especially reassuring to a pregnant woman who lost a baby to SIDS. She may be terrified it will happen again.
• Remember, especially in patient assessment, that SIDS can hurt the parents for a long time, and cause problems that surface months later in unexpected ways. Most parents need more help than you can reasonably provide. Give them the local SIDS Foundation's phone number. The Foundation offers professional follow-up support.

What is SIDS?

Sudden infant death syndrome, or SIDS, strikes infants largely between the ages of one week and one year. They die in their sleep, unexpectedly and usually without a struggle. The causes of SIDS are a mystery. Generally autopsies reveal:
—mild pulmonary congestion and edema
—intrathoracic petechiae
—minor pharyngeal edema

Laryngospasm is a suspected cause of death, but why it occurs is unknown. Infants of low birthweight seem most susceptible to the syndrome, particularly in winter.

Set the stage

When you're certain a patient won't survive, try to prepare the family for the inevitable. But wait for the doctor to warn them of the patient's condition. When the family asks you about the patient's health, reply honestly. Don't offer hope if none exists. For example, don't make ambiguous statements like, "He's got youth on his side" or "He's holding his own." Such remarks will only confuse the family. Instead, say something like, "Things don't look any better, but we'll keep you posted," or "His condition hasn't changed." Reinforce what the doctor's already told them, making sure your comments can't be misconstrued. A family may grasp any slender thread of hope you offer and later accuse you of misleading them.

Preparing family and friends for impending death helps them work out some of their grief feelings in advance. Hopefully, they can then cope with the actual death more easily.

When death happens suddenly

But what happens when death occurs suddenly, and you haven't time to ease survivors into the crisis situation? For example, suppose the city fire department brings in a 70-year-old man who collapsed and died while playing golf. His family must be called in to identify the body. The man had never been a patient at your hospital. What's more, his family doctor doesn't have staff privileges there. What can you do?

If you must contact the family to come to the hospital, stay calm and try to keep them calm. Never announce by phone that a loved one is dead—especially when the death was unexpected. However, don't state his condition in a way that bewilders them. For example, don't say, "I'm sorry to tell you this, but your husband is here. Can you come to the hospital right away?" Instead, say, "Mrs. Arthur? This is Mary Hanley at the Boro Hospital. Your husband is seriously ill. Please come to the emergency department as soon as possible. Can someone drive you here?" (Her answer to the question may tell you something about her support systems. If she has no one to turn to, she'll need that balancing factor strengthened.)

Don't alarm her. More than one survivor has been in a serious accident while rushing to the hospital. If necessary, get your social services department to escort her or call the police, if they perform this service.

When family members arrive, instruct the staff member

Calling the coroner
Notify your local medical examiner—or get someone else to do it—when:
• death is sudden and unattended by the patient's doctor.
• the patient's from another state.
• the patient dies within 48 hours after admission (unless his illness is diagnosed as terminal upon admittance).
• the patient committed suicide; was involved in a homicide; or an event of a criminal nature.
And in some states when:
• the patient will be cremated.
• the patient was a minor.

RELIGIOUS BELIEFS SURROUNDING HEALTH CRISIS AND DEATH

RELIGIOUS GROUP	BELIEFS AND PRACTICES SURROUNDING HEALTH CRISES	BELIEFS AND PRACTICES SURROUNDING DEATH
Seventh-Day Adventist	Communion. Anointing with oil. Baptism by immersion.	Dead are only asleep until Christ's return.
Armenian	Communion by the advocate. Laying on of hands.	Holy Communion is the last rite.
Baha'i	Prayer and fasting, if medically permissible.	No last rites.
Baptist	Baptism of believers by immersion. Laying on of hands.	Clergy prays with family.
Buddhism	Contact Buddhist priest for patient counseling, if the family requests it.	Contact priest. Last rite chanting at bedside. Body cremated.
Black Muslim	Don't believe in faith healing. Don't consider faith essential for healing.	Special procedure for washing and shrouding the dead.
Christian Scientist	Deny existence of health crisis. Can call Christian Scientist practitioner to administer spiritual support.	No last rites. No autopsy. Burial or cremation.
Church of Christ	Baptism by immersion after age 8. Communion. Anointing of oil and laying on of hands by minister.	No last rites.
Church of God	Divine healing through prayer.	No last rites. No cremation.
Church of Jesus Christ of Latter Day Saints (Mormons)	Divine healing through laying on of hands. Call priest to administer Sacrament of Last Supper, usually on Sundays.	Baptism of dead. Cremation discouraged. Preaching of Gospel to dead.
Eastern Orthodox	Anointing the sick.	Last rites in impending death. Cremation discouraged.
Episcopal	Baptism urgent when newborn baby's likely to die. Some believe in spiritual healing.	Last rites not mandatory. Check with family.
Friends (Quakers)	Individual decision.	Individual decision.
Grace Brethren	Anointing with oil for physical healing and/or spiritual uplifting.	No last rites. Individual decision on burial.
Greek Orthodox	Priest gives Holy Communion. Patient may request Sacrament of Holy Unction.	Sacrament of Holy Communion considered last rites. Discourage autopsies and cremation.

RELIGIOUS BELIEFS SURROUNDING HEALTH CRISIS AND DEATH

RELIGIOUS GROUP	BELIEFS AND PRACTICES SURROUNDING HEALTH CRISES	BELIEFS AND PRACTICES SURROUNDING DEATH
Hindu	Loss of limb represents sins committed in previous life.	Call in priest in impending death. Don't remove the thread he'll probably tie around the patient's neck or wrist; it signifies a blessing. Priest pours water into corpse's mouth. Check with family about handling body.
Islam—Muslim/ Moslem	The imam (religious leader) is called to hear confession of sins. Religion doesn't permit removal of organs for transplant.	Family washes and prepares body for death. Face body toward Mecca. No autopsy.
Jehovah's Witnesses	Blood transfusions not permitted, because of Psalm 16 interpretation. Can obtain court ruling to give blood to child, overriding parents' decision.	No last rites.
Judaism	Donation or transplantation of body organs requires consultation with rabbi.	In case of impending death, patient or fellow Jew may read Psalms 23, 103, 139 aloud. Last words should be "Hear, O Israel, the Lord our God, the Lord is One." Burial within 24 hours. No burial on sabbath (Saturday). Attended by relative till buried.
Lutheran	Usually baptize infants before 8 weeks old. If prognosis poor, patient may request anointment and blessing.	Last rites optional.
Nazarene	Baptism is parents' option.	No last rites. Stillborns are buried.
Orthodox Presbyterian	Infant baptism. Communion.	Reading of scripture and prayer.
Roman Catholic	Infant baptism mandatory. Baptism of aborted fetus unless tissue necrosis is evident. Amputated limb buried in consecrated ground.	In impending death, call priest to administer the Rite of Anointing the Sick.
Russian Orthodox	Baptism by priest only. Do not shave male patient except in preparation for surgery.	No autopsy, embalming, or cremation. After death, arms are crossed with fingers set in cross. Clothing worn by dead must be of natural fiber.
Unitarian/Universalist	No official sacraments. Baptism by choice.	Cremation preferred.

Helping a child face sudden death

After a head-on collision, 8-year-old Danny Seigal is brought to the E.D. unconscious. Because he was sleeping on the back seat at the time of the accident, he wasn't badly hurt. But both his parents were killed. How can you help him?

• Make sure you're there when he wakes up. He'll realize something terrible's happened and will need someone to talk to.

• As soon as you think it's wise, tell him his parents are dead. Then to help ease his stress, find out how he perceives death. Ask if he's ever had a pet that died.

If he's coped with death before, he may understand it better than you'd expect.

• Ask what he's learned about death from his religious school teacher. Then reinforce his family's religious beliefs, no matter what you believe.

• Answer his questions honestly. *Never* say his parents are asleep or have gone away on a long trip.

• Make sure he doesn't blame himself for his parents' deaths. He may think that they died because he felt angry with them. But don't wait for him to share these feelings with you. Instead, say something like, "When I was your age, I'd sometimes get so mad at my parents that I'd wish they were dead. But feelings like that are normal and can't hurt anyone."

Of course, erasing all the pain a child has after a tragedy like Danny's isn't possible. But the right words, sensitively spoken, can provide lasting comfort.

who'll see them first to ask only essential questions. Then bring them to a quiet room to meet the doctor. There he can break the sad news and let them openly express their grief. Always let the doctor do this, because it reassures the family that their loved one had proper medical attention. But if one of the survivors asks you, "Is he dead?," before the doctor arrives, tell him the truth. Say something like, "Yes, he's dead. But, let me have the doctor explain the details."

As you know, emotional support is a crucial balancing factor. If only one family member appears, try to get the hospital chaplain or another clergyman to stay with him for awhile. Also, ask the survivor if you should call another family member or friend. Never leave the grieving person completely alone.

Practical ways to help

If you're like most nurses, you may have trouble standing by quietly as family members act out their grief. Perhaps you feel that unless you're doing something, you're not being helpful. Instead, think of yourself as a friend, not "the nurse." Reach out and put your arm around a family member's shoulders, or hold his hand. But look for his reaction to your touching; some people may resent contact.

Do you feel like crying along with them? Go ahead. However, exercise self-control. You have responsibilities to the family. Just being there may be the most helpful thing you can do. Later, enlist the assistance of a volunteer to get coffee or make phone calls.

What about religious beliefs? Religion helps many people cope with death. Faith in a Supreme Being can be a strong supporting mechanism. Always note the family's religion, in case they'll want certain rites performed. (For details on how religious customs and beliefs about death vary, see page 64.)

Should the family see the body? In most cases, yes. However, if the body was mutilated, as in a plane or car crash, prepare the survivors ahead of time for what they'll see. Make sure the body is as clean and presentable as possible. Obviously, seeing the body will be difficult for survivors. But, it may be necessary to help them accept the death as a reality.

Should grieving survivors be sedated? Perhaps. But, even if the doctor has prescribed sedatives, think twice before you administer them. Remember, sedatives may quiet a person, but quieting him only postpones his grief. Consider, too, that

"If a child's coped with death before, he may understand it better than you'd expect. Don't underestimate his ability to deal with it."

a grieving family member may be allergic to certain medications and forget or ignore this fact in his anguish.

Remember: You must report all sudden deaths to the local medical examiner and police, unless the patient's doctor was present at the time of death. You must also report all deaths occurring within 48 hours of admission, except for terminal illnesses.

Keep in mind that no matter how distressing it is, survivors might have to speak to these authorities to supply information. Don't alarm them. Say something like: "Since your husband died so suddenly, the cause is hard to determine immediately. It requires investigation. Your insurance company may need more details."

Going home
Going home after such an ordeal will be hard for the survivors. Strengthen their balancing factors by following these guidelines:

• Before the survivor leaves, give him all the patient's personal belongings, other than clothing which the coroner may need. In the rush of events, don't upset the survivor further by misplacing or forgetting something of real sentimental value to him. Document what you give to the coroner.

• If a close family member of the victim lives alone, try to have someone waiting for him at home. You never know when a grieving person will attempt suicide. Those who have lost a loved one this way are particularly likely to try it themselves.

• If you think the survivor will need additional help or counseling when he leaves the hospital, give him the phone number of the hospital's social service department.

• If possible, have your hospital contact survivors about a month after the death. No doubt, the family will appreciate your concern. Your call also gives them the chance to ask questions about things that may have been bothering them. Your answers will help relieve lingering stress.

Be flexible
When death has been sudden, try to be as accommodating and flexible as you can with survivors. You can never predict a person's mechanisms for coping. Barring extremes, allow him to use them.

However, expect different reactions to sudden death. For example, when a gypsy child died in our E.D., we placed the body in a private room. A large family of gypsies came to view it. Their grief was noisy and disrupted our routine. They cried, fell upon the body, and insisted on performing a special ritual. But when they left, we felt sure they accepted the death as reality and could cope with it effectively.

Another time, a young woman and her fiance were rushed in after an automobile accident. The woman was treated and released, but her fiance was dead on arrival. The next morning, her only memory of the accident was of being taken to the hospital after the crash. Her friends didn't know how to tell her that her fiance had died, so they brought her back to us. When she heard that her fiance was dead, she calmly said, "I knew it, but I didn't want to believe it. He was one of the good ones." She stayed with us to cry and talk for an hour. Then her friends took her home.

On still another occasion, the wife of the man who had collapsed while playing golf came to thank us for all we had done to try to save his life. She said she was glad he died doing something he enjoyed so much.

Your feelings about death

Wherever you work, you may have to help someone cope with sudden death someday. To deal with death and its aftermath effectively, first confront your own feelings about it. Does a patient's sudden death discourage you? Make you angry? Sadden you? Or is it a learning experience, which will ultimately prove rewarding?

Do the circumstances surrounding a sudden death change your feelings? Ask yourself: Would you find it easier to care for a young child hit by a car or a middle-aged man who suffered a fatal heart attack? Or suppose the victim reminds you of a loved one? How will you react? If you're very upset, you may have to ask another nurse to relieve you.

How do you feel about the survivors? Who would you find it easier to console? The mother of a burglar who was killed by a police bullet? Or the mother whose child drowned in the lake? Do you ever wonder how you'd react in their place?

How do you express your feelings? Sometimes it's easier to put them aside and say: "I'll get all the paperwork that's necessary completed." Before you do, recognize that you may be using your nursing role to avoid thinking about death. Remember that you pass through a grieving process each time

Kidney donations

When the family of a fatal accident victim decides to donate his kidneys, how do you react? Kidney donation is a morally and emotionally charged issue. The way you and other nurses respond to it will affect your nursing care. Watch what you say and do while tissue-typing results are being processed and the victim's being mechanically sustained. Give the surviving family the support they need by following these guidelines:

• Treat the patient as a person. Refer to him by name.

• Continue to give supportive care to the patient's entire body—not just to his kidneys. Give attention to his skin, mouth, gown, bedding.

• When you speak to the family, refer to the ventilator as life-sustaining, not lifesaving. Never use the term "keeping him alive."

• Lengthen visiting hours, but limit visitors to immediate family and clergy.

you confront death. Eventually, you'll have to face your feelings, no matter what they are. Sharing them with your co-workers may help you gain perspective

In recent years, much has been written on feelings about death. You can explore the subject fully by reading the Nursing Skillbook *Dealing with Death and Dying*. Remember, separation by death is a highly stressful and crisis-prone situation. But by understanding the grieving process—and showing some sensitivity—you can do much to soften death's impact on the survivor and yourself.

Where to refer the patient and his family

Encourage the survivors of sudden death to turn to their church, local social groups, or community activities to help them overcome their grief. For parents who've lost an infant to SIDS, give them a list of the following organizations:
• **National SIDS Foundation, Suite 1904, 310 South Michigan Avenue, Chicago, Ill. 60604. Phone: 312-663-0650**
• **The International Guild for Infant Survival, 1800 M Street NW, Washington, D.C. 20037. Phone: 202-833-2253**

For parents who've lost a child of any age, tell them about:
• **The Society of the Compassionate Friends, P.O. Box 181LV, Lathrup Village, Mich. 48076. Phone: 313-647-5226**

You can learn more about how to deal with the survivors of sudden death by writing:
• **The Center of Death Education and Research, University of Minnesota, 1167 Social Science Building, Minneapolis, Minn. 55455.**

5

Dealing with the confused patient

BY KRISTINE KRONER, RN, BSN

YOU'RE THE CHARGE NURSE on duty one night on the medical/ surgical unit. And you've just remarked that things seem relatively peaceful, considering how many patients you have. Suddenly a tremulous voice shatters the silence: "Arthur, Arthur! Come...help...me!" You jump to your feet, and rush toward room 309.

When you enter the room, you discover 82-year-old Edna Fleming on the floor, her gown spattered with blood from a disconnected I.V. line. Her nasogastric tube and Foley catheter—with its balloon still inflated—remain on the bed amid crumpled sheets. Only the side rails are as you left them: raised. As you approach, Mrs. Fleming shrinks back in terror. "You're not my son," she says. "What are you doing in my house?"

Sound familiar? Most of us have encountered situations like this—confusion or disorientation among patients. It's commonplace, particularly late at night in hospitals.

Is every such patient in crisis? How can you help someone like Mrs. Fleming? You can't even tell what's causing her confusion at first. But she obviously needs attention. If situations like this scare you, you need to read this chapter. In

Is there a physical cause for your patient's confusion?

Being alone in strange surroundings may not be the only reason your patient's confused. Confusion may also stem from any of the following physical conditions:

• alcohol withdrawal syndrome
• acute infection
• head trauma
• increased intracranial pressure
• cerebral or pulmonary emboli
• fluid and electrolyte disorders; for example, acute renal shutdown, hyponatremia, hypoglycemia, hypovolemia, or acidosis.

On the opposite side of this page you'll see a list of drugs that can cause confusion. Study it carefully.

Important: Regard confusion as a sign that something's wrong. Trying to treat it without first finding its cause is dangerous.

it, I'll give you practical advice on the following:

• How to recognize the confused patient, or one who may become confused.

• How to determine if she's actually in crisis.

• How to establish quick rapport with the patient who feels threatened.

• How to plan and implement interventions to relieve confusion (with or without the patient's help).

• How to prevent future confusion once the patient's equilibrium is restored.

Put yourself in Mrs. Fleming's place

To help you understand why some (but not all) patients become confused, let's take a closer look at Mrs. Fleming. Put yourself in her place right after she's transferred to your unit, and try to imagine how she feels being hospitalized.

Most likely, she's frightened. Instead of being safe at home with her unmarried son and her cat, she's lying in a strange hospital bed with tubes coming from her nose, arm, and bladder. Earlier that day, she was rushed to the emergency department with nausea and stomach pains. Later, the doctors told her she needed surgery, as soon as possible, for an intestinal obstruction.

Mrs. Fleming tells herself she's going to die. After all, isn't that why most people go to the hospital? She's seen it happen before. Soon she asks the nurse for a drink of water and gets told she's not permitted anything by mouth. That must mean she's getting worse! They'd better call her son, Arthur!

Too uncomfortable around strangers to share her fears, Mrs. Fleming shifts them uneasily in her mind. However, as the night deepens, she eventually falls asleep (with the help of a sedative). Then unexpectedly she awakens at 3 a.m. and doesn't remember where she is.

You get the picture. Confused and terrified, Mrs. Fleming yanks out the tubes she thinks are holding her in bed and climbs over the side rails. When she falls, she calls for her son, Arthur, and gets you instead. No *wonder* you frighten her. She doesn't know *who* you are.

What's your first step?

Before you read further, study the example on this page to see what causes confusion. Understanding the possible causes will help you in two ways: to prevent confusion, whenever possible, and to manage it effectively when it occurs.

As you already know from Chapters 1 and 2, your first step is assessment. How do you identify the patient who's confused or about to become confused? Start by investigating puzzling or bizarre behavior.

For example, does the patient call you by an unfamiliar name? Say: "My name is Margaret. Tell me who Janet is." Don't say: "There's no one here but me, Mr. Smith. You're confused again."

When a patient's behaving oddly, ask questions that'll elicit only *useful* information. If you simply say: "How are you feeling?" to a man who suddenly starts staring at the wall, he may answer "Fine." Instead, ask "What do you see over there, Mr. Gibbs?" That may get a specific answer.

Never assume bizarre behavior always accompanies confusion. A patient may appear content and quiet, but still be completely disoriented. Do you notice subtle, but disturbing changes in the way he acts? Ask a question that'll reveal possible confusion. Say: "What are your plans after lunch?" He may answer "To wash the ants off these dishes."

Sometimes a patient has alternating periods of confusion and lucidity. For example, he may easily become disoriented when he's alone in the dark. But when you turn on the light and ask him where he is, he may suddenly remember he's in the hospital.

Always suspect confusion—or impending confusion—when the patient:
• becomes increasingly restless or apprehensive
• doesn't respond to your questions and has difficulty concentrating
• shows sensitivity to noise and light
• has nightmares or insomnia
• acts bewildered; has trouble identifying people correctly
• shows marked fluctuations in mood, actions, and rationality
• strokes or picks at the bed linen, or at air
• has frequent crying or laughing spells
• seems preoccupied much of the time, acting jumpy and irritable when disturbed.

Important: Thoroughly investigate each sign and symptom. Don't assume confusion's causing everything, even though the patient's been confused before. Review the medications he's

Is a drug causing your patient's confusion?

When investigating the source of your patient's confusion, don't overlook the possibility that his medication may be responsible. Here's a list of drugs whose side-effects may include confusion:
• acetazolamide (Diamox)
• amphetamines
• atropine
• barbiturates
• carbamazepine (Tegretol)
• chloramphenicol (Chloromycetin)
• chlordiazepoxide (Librium)
• droperidol (Inapsine)
• flurazepam (Dalmane)
• imipramine (Tofranil)
• indomethacin (Indocin)
• insulin
• isocarboxazid (Marplan)
• ketamine (Ketalar)
• procainamide (Pronestyl)
  Note when confusion occurs. Does it coincide with the peak action period of a drug? Document your observations and bring them to the doctor's attention.

HOW SENSORY OVERLOAD CAUSES CONFUSION

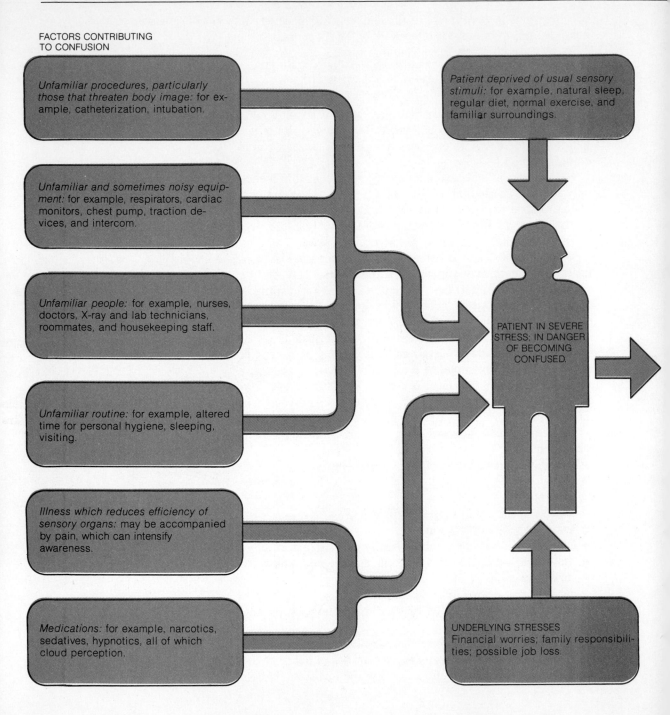

FACTORS CONTRIBUTING
TO CONFUSION

Unfamiliar procedures, particularly those that threaten body image: for example, catheterization, intubation.

Unfamiliar and sometimes noisy equipment: for example, respirators, cardiac monitors, chest pump, traction devices, and intercom.

Unfamiliar people: for example, nurses, doctors, X-ray and lab technicians, roommates, and housekeeping staff.

Unfamiliar routine: for example, altered time for personal hygiene, sleeping, visiting.

Illness which reduces efficiency of sensory organs: may be accompanied by pain, which can intensify awareness.

Medications: for example, narcotics, sedatives, hypnotics, all of which cloud perception.

Patient deprived of usual sensory stimuli: for example, natural sleep, regular diet, normal exercise, and familiar surroundings.

PATIENT IN SEVERE STRESS; IN DANGER OF BECOMING CONFUSED.

UNDERLYING STRESSES
Financial worries; family responsibilities; possible job loss.

Unrealistic perception: Patient forgets what time it is, where he is, and why he's there. He may fail to recognize familiar faces.

Unrealistic perception: Patient has difficulty concentrating, setting valid priorities, and understanding necessary procedures.

Ineffective coping: Patient begins to have nightmares, fantasies, and hallucinations.

Ineffective coping: Patient may become argumentative, hysterical, withdrawn, anxious, or combative.

Unavailable supports: Patient no longer communicates well with family, friends, or health-care professionals.

Unavailable supports: Patient no longer sees nurse as a supportive person; instead he regards her as a threat to his well-being.

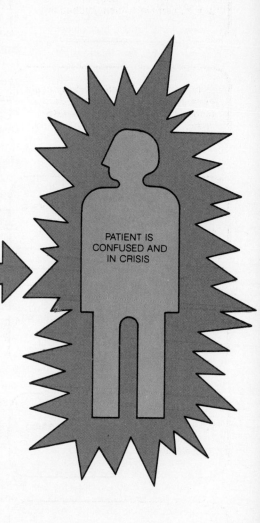

PATIENT IS
CONFUSED AND
IN CRISIS

Post-code confusion

If you've ever cared for a patient after a successful resuscitation, you know he may temporarily be extremely confused. Commonly called "post-code confusion," this condition adds to his stress. How can you help?

• Use reality-oriented techniques to reduce his confusion. For example, explain his condition: "Your heart wasn't doing its job, so we had to stimulate it." Touch him—be his contact with life.

• Reduce his anxiety by explaining why he's in pain. Use simple terms. Say: "That burning sensation on your chest is caused by the machine we used to make your heart work right again."

• Speak softly in one-thought sentences. Remember, he probably has difficulty concentrating. Don't overtax his attention span.

• Refuse to argue with him if he becomes belligerent; you'll only agitate him further.

• Shield him from unnecessary stress. Have him choose one or two close friends and relatives he'd like to see, then limit his other visitors. Respect his privacy whenever possible.

• Remember, many patients who've been successfully resuscitated recall the episode with striking accuracy, so don't assume that this phenomenon indicates confusion. Encourage him to talk about it. Document what he tells you in your notes.

Important: Resuscitation isn't the only thing that can cause post-code confusion. It may also be triggered by any severe electric shock: for example, lightning.

taking to see if confusion's a side effect. Check his vital signs, neurologic status, fluid and electrolyte balance, and blood urea nitrogen (BUN). He may have a physical disorder that needs the doctor's attention.

In crisis or not in crisis?

Is the confused patient in crisis? Probably, if the onset was sudden and you can't quickly reorient him. To find out, continue to follow the assessment guidelines in Chapter 1.

First, try to discover if his confusion was triggered by some *specific stressful event.* You may find this difficult to do at first because a confused patient usually can't tell you much. Talk it over with the other nurses and review the causes for confusion. But don't waste valuable time trying to pinpoint a *specific* triggering event at that point; hopefully you can do that later. Go on to the next step, and *work quickly.*

Assess the patient's balancing factors. Which ones are absent or need strengthening? If he's completely confused, he may be missing all three balancing factors. If he's only slightly confused, he may simply need them strengthened. Ask yourself:

• *Does this patient perceive the triggering event realistically?* Obviously, he's not perceiving much of anything realistically if he's completely confused. However, when and if lucidity returns, he may remember being confused. Try to talk to him about it then to determine what triggered it. (For specific tips on what to say when you discuss his confusion, see page 87.)

• *Does he have adequate emotional supports? Are they available to him now?* If you and the other nurses are the patient's only available supports, you'll probably notice that he becomes less confused the minute you appear. Spend as much time as possible with him.

• *Are his coping mechanisms working effectively?* Probably not, or he'd have retained his grip on reality. After you've reoriented him, talk to him. Try to find out how he usually copes with stress. Then give him a chance to use those mechanisms, when possible—or help him find alternatives.

Back to reality

Now that you've completed your assessment, try to make contact with your patient so you can reorient him to reality. Making contact comes before establishing rapport. Expect

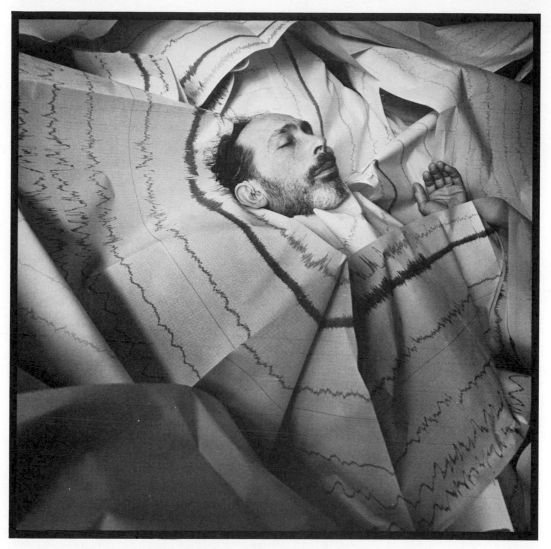

"After a brush with death, the resuscitated patient may suffer post-code confusion. When he does, the added stress puts his equilibrium in jeopardy."

some difficulties, particularly if your patient feels threatened.

Here are some guidelines:

• Try to stay calm, no matter what's happened. Take care not to startle him, particularly if he's been confused before, if he's alone in the dark, if he's recovering from anesthesia, or if he's receiving sedatives.

• Never assume the patient's asleep just because his eyes are closed. This is important; he may be feigning sleep in hopes you'll go away.

• Speak clearly and distinctly, and call him by name. So you won't seem threatening, get as close to his eye level as possible.

• Approach cautiously. Gently touch his hand or shoulder. If he pulls back, wait and try again. However, maintain some kind of contact with him; for example, put your hand on the bed. Keep your hands visible at all times. If he strikes you, summon help immediately. Use the emergency call light. Don't leave the patient alone. (For further tips on how to deal with the combative patient, see pages 82 to 85.)

• Make sure he can see, hear, and talk to you. Turn on the lights. Restore his glasses, hearing aid, and dentures, if any. Eliminate all unnecessary stimuli; for example, turn off the TV set. Pull the curtain for privacy; ask visitors to leave.

• Try to make the patient comfortable. Take care of any immediate problems he may have; for example, a disconnected I.V. tube. If the patient still seems restless, look for other problems. Does he keep kicking off the sheets? He may imagine giant spiders crawling in his bed. Or he may be trying to tell you he's too warm.

• Ask questions that'll elicit useful information. But keep them simple. For example, say: "You're having a rough time tonight, Mr. O'Malley. What can I do to help?" Don't say: "You're confused again, Mr. O'Malley. Just look at the mess you've made of this bed."

• If you must give instructions, do so slowly and distinctly. Avoid sounding threatening. Never say something like: "I'm going to tell your doctor if you don't lie still," or "Your son will be upset when I tell him about all the trouble you're causing for us."

• Stay with the patient—or get someone else to stay with him—until he's calm and reoriented. Remember, he may become confused again. Before you leave, make sure the side rails are up. Get an order for restraints, if necessary.

Continue your interventions

Have you made contact with your patient and reoriented him to reality? Confusion can easily recur, so plan and implement interventions to help prevent it. Set realistic goals to replace or strengthen his balancing factors. For example, try to establish a set routine he can count on. Unpredictable changes and constant variations in day-to-day care upset a confused patient and may throw him into panic.

If possible, let the patient help you plan interventions that'll minimize his confusion. But don't assume you can successfully reorient every patient to the point where he can discuss his care. Some (like those with organic brain disease) may never be lucid. In such cases, you'll need extra patience to discover and relieve hidden stresses, maintain a reality-oriented relationship, and work within his limitations.

To help you, I'll discuss ways you can reduce the stress of any confused patient.

Get off to a good start

Do your best to establish and maintain a reality-oriented relationship from the very start. Make sure the patient understands where he is, why he's there, and approximately what will happen to him.

Begin by assuming he's frightened, because he probably is. He's scared of being hospitalized, of strange tests and equipment, and of unfamiliar nurses and doctors. Now, ask yourself what he'll encounter during his hospital stay: what noises and activities he'll hear and see, what tests and procedures he'll have, and which people he'll meet. Relieve his fears by explaining what to expect in words he'll understand.

Try to find out what being in the hospital means to him. Ask: "When was the last time you were in a hospital? What was it like? What things do you remember about it?" He may say that being hospitalized makes him feel helpless. Or he may think it means he's going to die. If you can, reduce these anxieties by reassuring him. Spend a few minutes talking to him, so he'll remember you as someone he can trust.

During your initial assessment, determine the patient's usual routine. For example, does he regularly watch television, go for a walk, take an afternoon nap? If possible try to fit these activities into his care plan. But if you can't, try to find out what he can substitute for these coping mechanisms.

COPING WITH THE COMBATIVE PATIENT

What makes a patient suddenly combative? Can you spot the verbal and nonverbal cues that identify him as potentially combative? How can you intervene at that point to keep his aggression in check? Suppose your interventions fail, and your patient gets out of control? If you're not sure how to protect yourself, him, and others, you need to read this section.

Acting out frustrations

First, let's examine what can make a patient combative. As you know, when a patient's usual coping mechanisms break down under stress, he becomes frustrated and, in many cases, angry. If his customary response to angry feelings is to act them out, then his behavior may become aggressive. Far from seeing you as a care-giver, he may see you as a threat, an obstacle, or an enemy.

Think of combative behavior this way: The patient is responding in anger to a situation he can't cope with. In many cases, he's confused. For example, a patient may become combative because of a nursing measure like wrist restraints that he doesn't understand. Such a measure becomes the triggering factor that puts him in crisis.

Recognizing the precombative patient

The best way to deal with combative behavior is to anticipate it and intervene before the situation gets out of control. Watch for unusual behavior that identifies the potentially combative patient. For instance, does he:
• seem elated, restless, agitated?
• demand constant attention from everyone?

• talk loudly or boisterously?
• tease and bait others constantly with sarcasm?
• pepper his conversation with vulgarities and profanities?
• show a limited attention span?

Remember, what the frustrated, angry patient needs most is not to suppress these troublesome feelings, but to free himself of them by expressing them. Help him do this, if you can, while protecting him from hurting himself or others.

Channel aggression

If your patient's behavior suggests he may become combative:
• Place someone in charge of decision-making. If the patient

has to be forcefully restrained, someone will have to decide when all other forms of intervention have failed.
• Choose someone who'll relate best to the patient to do the interacting. This might be a favorite nurse, an aide, or doctor.

Let's assume you're that person. What do you do? First, identify the patient's immediate problem and try to relieve the pressure. Remember the claustrophobic patient back in Chapters 1 and 2? By lowering his side rails, the nurse removed the source of his panic. Look for the triggering factor, then take appropriate measures to lower your patient's stress level.

You won't always find it that

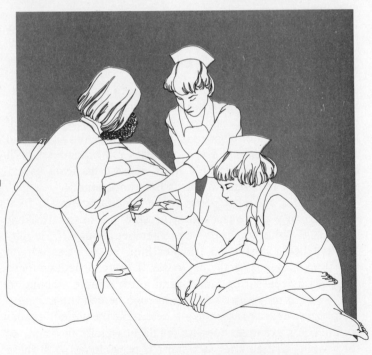

You may have to restrain a patient long enough to give him a sedative. Use your weight to pin his torso and legs to the bed.

easy to deal with an impending crisis, but the principle still applies. To illustrate, imagine yourself face to face with 50-year-old Mr. Palmer, who suddenly overturns his food tray, shouts "I'm leaving!" and heads for the elevator, trailing a stream of oaths. What do you do?

First, recognize that he's asking for help. Don't try to stop him physically. Instead, try to find out why he wants to leave. By doing so you divert his energy, and get him to focus on the immediate problem, which you may be able to remedy.

Encourage communication
Remember, you're dealing with the patient's actions, not his personality. Listen to him, but don't take provocative remarks or abusive language personally. Try not to show disapproval, even when it's difficult. Don't use complex ideas or involved explanations; speak in short sentences. Make decisions, but don't feel obliged to explain.

Control your nonverbal messages: They should reinforce what you say, not contradict it. For example, maintain eye contact. Don't look around the room while the patient's talking. Let him know he has your complete attention.

Watch your posture. Keep it relaxed. Don't look aggressive or defensive. *Important:* Use gestures carefully. Smiling, nod-

ding, and other "positive" gestures sometimes communicate the opposite of what you intend. An agitated patient may misinterpret your smile and think you're laughing at him.

Dealing with combative behavior
Suppose you fail to recognize the patient who's about to become combative, and he starts acting out.

Your first aim's still communication, but this time the patient, not you, will be in control. Only by correctly responding to his signals can you regain the control necessary to resolve his crisis. To help you do this, here are some guidelines:

• Call for assistance. However, ask the others to stay out of sight or very much in the background. Make sure they know what you're doing at all times.
• Minimize stimuli. Turn off TV; close doors; and clear the area. Assign someone to remove other patients and visitors, quietly and without unnecessary explanations.
• Protect yourself. Observe your position in relation to the door, to any weapons in the room, and to possible escape routes. *Never* turn your back.
• Don't be authoritarian. Avoid threats, raised voices, pulling rank.
• Test your progress. As you move closer, watch the patient's reaction. Be aware of his need for personal space; approach cautiously.
• Continue to communicate. Listen and respond with empathy. You can make deals, but be honest. Don't make promises you don't intend to carry out.
• Be prepared to use restraints. Know what the person in charge is going to do if other methods fail.

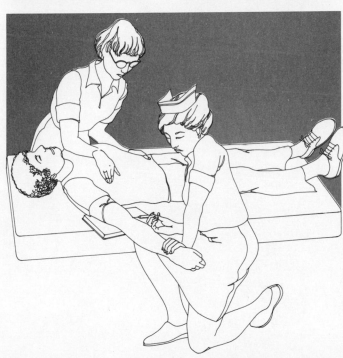

When you give an I.V. injection to a combative patient, brace his arm so he can't bend his elbow. Protect yourself by stooping beside bed.

BASIC SELF-DEFENSE

Suppose you must physically protect yourself from a combative patient. Knowing how to escape from commonly-used holds could save you from injury. Study these simple, effective self-defense methods. Then, practice them with other health-team members.

Escaping from a wrist-hold:

Imagine that the patient grabs your wrist as in Figure A. To escape, quickly bend your wrist and arm toward your body in one continuous motion, twisting your wrist outwards against the patient's thumb (Figure B).

Is he using both hands to hold your wrist (Figure C)? With your free hand, grab your other hand and pull it sharply toward your body. As Figure D shows, you pull *against* the patient's thumb, the weakest part of the grip.

Escaping from a choke-hold

If the patient applies pressure *from behind,* as in Figure E, do this: Bend at the waist and twist yourself around so you're facing the assailant. Then, follow through with the hand-clasp maneuver as above.
If the patient applies pressure *from the front,* as in Figure F, clasp your hands between yourself and the patient, below arm level. Then quickly raise your clasped hands and follow through until they're above your head (Figure G).

Note: You don't have to be physically stronger than the patient to make these techniques work. For success, however, you must perform them quickly and smoothly. Don't give him the chance to counter with more force. Practice until you can perform all moves swiftly and efficiently.

—BARBARA STITELER, RN

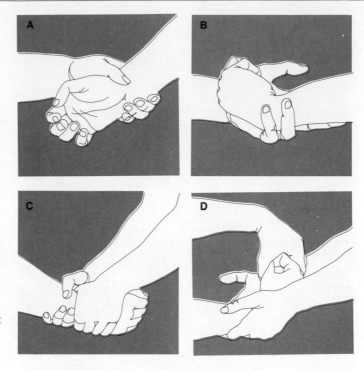

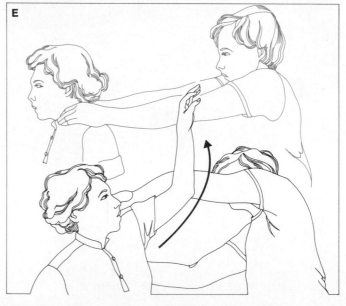

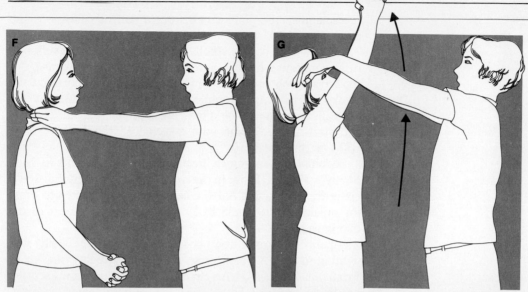

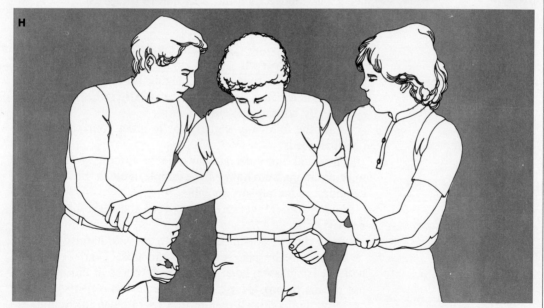

A two-person escort

This technique's useful for moving the patient to a safe area. It requires two people, and works best with a patient who's not too resistive.

Approach the patient, one person on each side. Suppose you're on the patient's right side:
1) Slide your left arm under his right, just above his elbow (see Figure H); 2) With your right hand, grab the patient's right wrist; 3) Grasp your right wrist with your left hand.

Remember, the more you disrupt a patient's life-style, the more likely he is to become confused.

Take the case of Mrs. Shelly, who came to our unit suffering from congestive heart failure and organic brain disease. Although she was told to stay in bed, the first two mornings she awoke at 5 a.m., got completely dressed, and came out into the hall. Once there, she'd look around, become visibly upset and start crying. "Who took my chair?" she'd wail. "How will I get my breakfast?"

Fortunately, our quick investigation put an end to Mrs. Shelly's distress. From her records, we discovered that she'd come from a nursing home where she was expected to dress for breakfast, sit in the hall, and wait for an escort to the dining room.

Already in stress from hospitalization, Mrs. Shelly was fighting to keep a small grasp on the only reality she knew. From that day on, we left a chair outside her room and escorted her to the lounge each morning before breakfast.

That safe feeling

By creating a comfortable, nonthreatening environment for your patient, you can relieve or possibly prevent recurrent confusion. To do this, try to imagine how you'd feel in his circumstances. Then do what you can to strengthen his support systems by altering the environment.

Adapt the following suggestions to meet your patient's individual needs:

• Surround him with familiar objects. Encourage his family to bring things from home: for example, a clock, photographs, calendar, radio, afghan, or bible.

Nursing tip: Make sure you record these on his personal property sheet.

• Open the curtains in his room to provide natural light.

• Make sure he can see, hear, and talk. Don't leave him without his glasses, hearing aid, or dentures, if any. Does he use a cane or prosthesis? Make sure he has it nearby.

• Move the confused patient to a room close to the nurses' station, if possible. But never restrain him in a chair by your desk to watch him. Both he and his family will find this humiliating.

• Make frequent checks, especially at night. To help, leave the patient's intercom on so you can monitor him. However,

CONVERSATION

As you know, reality orientation can help you reverse your patient's confusion. However, by using these conversation tips, you may do more than that; you may prevent confusion before it starts. To help, remember these general guidelines:

- Talk in simple phrases and give simple directions.
- Don't shout. Your patient's hearing isn't the problem.
- Communicate through an interpreter when the patient speaks a foreign language.

GENERAL GUIDELINES	WHEN HE SAYS	DON'T SAY	SAY:
Emphasize positive features of behavior.	"I caused a lot of problems last night, didn't I?"	"You really kept the night girls busy."	"You seem okay now. What do you remember?"
Avoid making threatening statements.	"My sister's out on the roof. I have to save her."	"If you don't stop it, we'll transfer you to the psych unit."	"You're in the hospital Mrs. March. Are you worried about your sister?"
Don't make false promises.	"Take these handcuffs off! I want out of here."	"If you calm down, we'll take off your restraints."	"Mr. Ames, you're in the hospital and your arms are restrained so you don't remove your tubes."
Never use medical abbreviations.	"I want a drink of water."	"You can't have one now, Mr. Jansen. You're NPO after midnight."	"Mr. Jansen, your operation's tomorrow morning and you're not allowed to drink anything after midnight."
Don't ignore what your patient says.	"Have you got a knife to cut these ropes?"	"I have to tend other patients now."	"They aren't ropes Mr. Ellis. Your arms are restrained so you won't climb out of bed."
	WHEN A FAMILY MEMBER SAYS:	DON'T SAY:	INSTEAD, SAY:
Don't be judgmental. Let the family express their feelings.	"Dad, if you don't stop talking like this, I won't come back."	"Don't threaten your father."	"Please come out in the hall for a few minutes, so I can explain your father's condition."

Confused child

The confused child needs your immediate help. Without prompt intervention, his confusion can intensify and possibly lead to coma or convulsions.

To determine if a child's confused, ask yourself:
• Does the child play the way you'd expect him to? Does he make up games or draw pictures to act out his feelings about hospitalization?
• How does he interact with his parents? Does he seem calmer when they're with him? If not, perhaps he doesn't recognize them.
• Does he follow instructions a child of his age should understand? Is his attention span appropriate for his age?
• Is he curious about his environment?
• Does he react like a typical child to hospital procedures? For example, does he cry when you give him an injection?
• Does he know who he is, where he is, and what day it is? Even when his routine has changed, he should know approximately when it's time to eat or take a nap.

You can lessen the child's stress by maintaining a supportive environment. Don't deprive him of play time, music, and other stimulation. Encourage him to talk and play with others, especially children his own age.

Surround him with comforting objects such as toys, stuffed animals, and books.

Encourage his parents to visit as much as possible. When they're away, talk to the child about them. Reassure him that they care.

avoid using the intercom to answer his calls. If he's already confused, doing so may confuse him further.
• Allow visitors to stay longer than usual. Familiar faces help the patient keep his grip on reality.
• Don't create situations that may worry your patient or make him suspicious. Avoid low-pitched conversations just outside his room.

Attend to his other needs

Promote natural sleep by letting your patient follow as nearly a normal routine as possible. Find out his usual sleep habits and try to accommodate them. Don't resort to sedatives unless absolutely necessary. Remember, medications increase the risk of confusion.

Give him the help he needs eating, drinking, and tending to personal hygiene. However, don't take over tasks he can do himself. Let him be as independent as possible, no matter how slow he is. Robbing him of his dignity would increase feelings of helplessness, intensify his frustration, and make him irritable.

If your patient refuses to eat or drink, try to find out why. He may have a reason you can do something about. To discover it, say: "You've left your breakfast and lunch untouched today, Mr. Rogers. What do you normally eat for these meals?" Never say: "What's wrong? Don't you like the food?" That sounds threatening and will make him defensive.

Occasionally a patient won't eat because the food looks strange to him. For example, he may have close ties to another country and prefer ethnic specialties. Or he may not recognize familiar foods because they're packaged differently. To a confused patient, gelatin may not look like gelatin if it's in a foil-covered paper cup.

Don't resort to I.V. fluids or feedings unless absolutely necessary.

Stick to a set routine, as much as possible. Don't be late with medications, procedures, or a promised backrub. Respect your patient's limitations. Don't expect too much from him, especially on days when his routine has been upset.

Discover hidden fears

As I mentioned earlier, knowing something about your patient's background, family life, and occupation will help you

"A confused child needs your help. Without prompt intervention, his confusion can intensify, possibly leading to coma or convulsions."

make contact with him when he's confused. This knowledge will also help you relieve many of his hidden fears and stresses.

For example, I once cared for an elderly patient who'd scream with fear when left alone at night. During those episodes, he was too confused to tell us anything useful. But we sensed his fears were somehow related to an occasionally used respirator at his bedside.

One night he screamed the name "Hitler" at the machine. An alert nurse, who knew he'd been in a concentration camp when he was younger, solved the puzzle. The design on the front of the respirator resembled a swastika. In his confusion, the patient thought he was back in the concentration camp. We immediately relieved this unnecessary stress by substituting another respirator.

No matter how senseless they sound, don't assume your patient's confused ramblings have no connection with reality. Look for clues by checking his occupation and background. For example, we had a patient in our unit who was frequently heard counting money. When we checked his former occupation, we discovered that he'd once been a turnpike toll collector. Knowing this enabled us to make contact with him during those confused episodes. We'd say: "You're not collecting tolls tonight, Mr. Miller. Tonight you're in the hospital."

Help the family
What about the confused patient's family? Have you given them the emotional support they need? In many cases, they won't know how to cope with their loved one's sudden confusion. And they may panic.

Expect some difficult situations. For example, they may decide you've caused your patient's confusion by keeping him up too long, restricting his diet in some way, or interrupting his sleep.

Never argue with family members. Instead, take them out of the patient's room and try to explain the situation. Describe the possible causes of confusion and reassure them that it's not uncommon. They're probably having trouble accepting the situation, so they coped by temporarily fixing the blame on you.

Teach the family how to react when the patient's confused. If you don't, they may scold him, which'll only make him worse. For example, does the patient sometimes think he's

DOCUMENTING CONFUSION

When you're documenting a confused or combative patient's behavior, be precise. Don't use vague terms or judgmental language. Instead of labeling his actions, describe them with specific details.

NURSE'S NOTES

DATE	TIME	DON'T WRITE	INSTEAD, WRITE
3/10/79	4 p.m.	Patient uncooperative.	Patient refuses to eat or speak.
		Patient confused.	Patient thinks he's at home and nurses are trespassing.
		Patient pulled out Foley.	Patient's Foley catheter found lying on bed with balloon inflated. No trauma noted. Patient has no memory of what happened.
	4:30 p.m.	Patient belligerent.	Patient becomes loudly argumentative when asked to walk in hall.
		Patient combative.	Patient strikes, spits and swings arms at anyone near him. Efforts to calm him verbally unsuccessful. Wrist restraints applied.
		Patient hallucinating.	Patient sees giant ants in his bed; tries to brush them off with his hands.

somewhere else? Urge the family not to argue with him. Tell them never to say: "Stop talking nonsense, Dad. You know perfectly well you're in the hospital." Instead, suggest they say: "I know you miss the farm. I miss it, too. But now, you're in the hospital, Dad."

A big challenge
Now let's assume you've done all you can to relieve your patient's stress, as well as his family's. Have you prevented or reduced further confusion? Evaluate the results of your interventions, using the guidelines in Chapter 2.

However, don't be discouraged if your plans fail sometimes. Working with a confused patient can be frustrating and discouraging.

Get support and relief when you need it from other nurses on your team. Enlist their aid for innovative approaches to relieve the patient's stresses and anxieties.

If you're confident that you eased at least some of his distress, you can feel you've helped him. The confused patient doesn't demand more than you can give. But he does need the best that you can offer.

Where to refer the patient and his family
When not caused by medication or disease, chronic confusion usually afflicts the elderly. Learn more about it. Write:
• The Gerontological Society, 1 Dupont Circle, Suite 520, Washington, D.C. 20036
• The National Geriatrics Society, 3rd Floor, 212 W. Wisconsin Avenue, Milwaukee, Wis. 53203.

6

Recognizing and protecting the suicidal patient

BY THERESA CROUSHORE, RN

WILL THE NEXT PATIENT you see commit suicide? Possibly, because suicide is the final option for anyone in stress, no matter what his age, race, sex, or socioeconomic status. But are you skilled enough to recognize him? Tragically, not all nurses or health-care professionals are.

Consider this startling fact: In almost 2 out of 3 of all suicide attempts, the victim had seen a health-care professional within the previous 3 months. If you'd been that professional, would you have realized he was suicidal? Could you have done anything to prevent his attempt? For example, can you recognize a suicidal patient's distress signals? Do you know which clues suggest suicide is imminent? Does the patient really want to kill himself?

Do you know the facts?
If questions like these leave you uncertain, you need to read this chapter. In it, I'll clear up dangerous misconceptions that'll keep you from recognizing the suicidal patient. I'll also tell you what to say to him and how to assess his balancing factors. And I'll explain how to refer him to an appropriate specialist without giving him the impression you're abandoning him.

When a child attempts suicide
Your suicidal patient may not be an adult. Among children under age 15, suicide is one of the leading causes of death. Don't assume your young patient's despair is trivial or transitory just because he's a child.

Here are some reasons he may attempt suicide:
• to escape abuse (especially sexual)
• to escape despair caused by thwarted goals, death or illness of loved one, loneliness, imagined inadequacies, or rejection by peers or parents
• to express fear or anger
• to manipulate quarreling or divorced parents.

When you're caring for a child who's attempted suicide, offer emotional support to him and his shocked and bewildered family. How you respond to their needs at this time may determine how they resolve their crisis.

Use these guidelines:
• Never blame the parents, no matter what you think of them. Chances are, they're already struggling with feelings of guilt or shame.
• Involve the family in your interventions. Encourage them to talk with the child about his anxieties. But don't rush it. Give them a chance to get over their initial anger and distress.
• Call the hospital's social service department to get specialized help for the child and his family.

Facts and fables

How many times have you heard statements like this about suicide: "Don't worry. He isn't the type to kill himself." Or "People who threaten suicide never really go through with it." Or "She made a halfhearted attempt at suicide once, but it was only to get attention."

Consider these remarks dangerous. They spread myths about suicide that can kill, because they keep others from taking the suicidal patient seriously. Unfortunately, these and other erroneous beliefs are still held by many otherwise well-informed people, including numerous health-care professionals.

Do you know the facts about suicide? Check the chart on page 97 and see. You may be surprised that some things you thought were true really aren't. Now imagine how many lay people have false notions, and you have some idea of the problem. Moreover, the natural tendency is to dismiss the possibility rather than confront it. Because no one recognizes the danger, thousands of suicide threats each year become reality.

Six danger signs

What can you do about it? Obviously, you can't clear up everyone's misconceptions and fears about suicide. But you can help in a big way by learning to recognize the danger signs. Make a quick assessment of your patient by asking yourself these questions:

• Has he threatened suicide? Has he hinted at it? Has he joked about it with friends?

• Has he ever attempted suicide before? Has he made even a halfhearted attempt?

• Does he have a history of reckless behavior? Does he seem unusually accident-prone?

• Does he seem depressed?

• Have you or others noticed a marked change in his behavior or personality?

• Does he act like he's given up on life? Has he been putting his affairs in order? Has he started giving away treasured personal possessions?

If you can answer *yes* to any of the above, your patient's life may be in jeopardy. Let's examine these danger areas more closely, so you know exactly what to look for when you make your initial assessment.

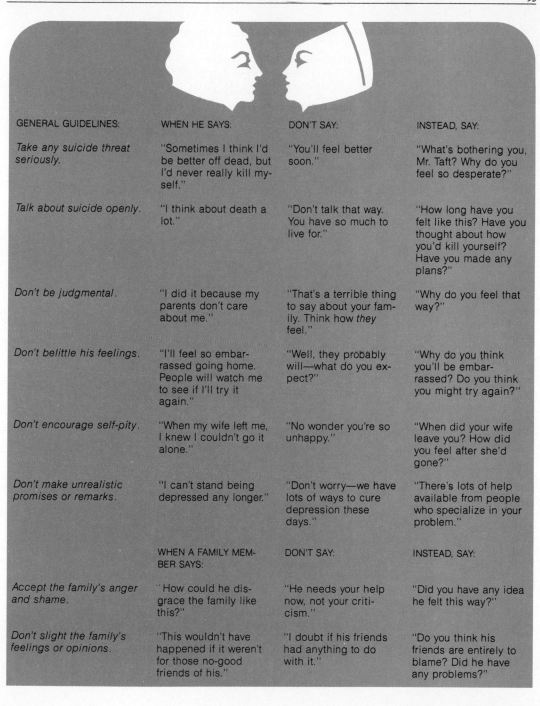

GENERAL GUIDELINES:	WHEN HE SAYS:	DON'T SAY:	INSTEAD, SAY:
Take any suicide threat seriously.	"Sometimes I think I'd be better off dead, but I'd never really kill myself."	"You'll feel better soon."	"What's bothering you, Mr. Taft? Why do you feel so desperate?"
Talk about suicide openly.	"I think about death a lot."	"Don't talk that way. You have so much to live for."	"How long have you felt like this? Have you thought about how you'd kill yourself? Have you made any plans?"
Don't be judgmental.	"I did it because my parents don't care about me."	"That's a terrible thing to say about your family. Think how *they* feel."	"Why do you feel that way?"
Don't belittle his feelings.	"I'll feel so embarrassed going home. People will watch me to see if I'll try it again."	"Well, they probably will—what do you expect?"	"Why do you think you'll be embarrassed? Do you think you might try again?"
Don't encourage self-pity.	"When my wife left me, I knew I couldn't go it alone."	"No wonder you're so unhappy."	"When did your wife leave you? How did you feel after she'd gone?"
Don't make unrealistic promises or remarks.	"I can't stand being depressed any longer."	"Don't worry—we have lots of ways to cure depression these days."	"There's lots of help available from people who specialize in your problem."
	WHEN A FAMILY MEMBER SAYS:	DON'T SAY:	INSTEAD, SAY:
Accept the family's anger and shame.	"How could he disgrace the family like this?"	"He needs your help now, not your criticism."	"Did you have any idea he felt this way?"
Don't slight the family's feelings or opinions.	"This wouldn't have happened if it weren't for those no-good friends of his."	"I doubt if his friends had anything to do with it."	"Do you think his friends are entirely to blame? Did he have any problems?"

HELPING THE DEPRESSED PATIENT

You don't have to work in a psychiatric unit to care for a depressed patient. Depression is so widespread that you may see it on a medical/surgical floor, in a clinic, or in a doctor's office.

As you probably know, unchecked depression is dangerous. It can cause a patient's stress level to become so intolerable that he may attempt suicide as a way to escape. How can you ease his mounting distress? This feature will tell you. But first, let's review what causes depression, as well as how to recognize it.

What causes depression?

In most cases, a patient becomes depressed because he's suffered some real or imagined loss: for example, a loved one, his job, or his body image. Expect temporary depression in a patient who's grieving because it's a normal part of the grieving process. And expect it with certain physical disorders; for example, Parkinson's disease or a fluid and electrolyte imbalance.

Certain medications can also cause depression in some patients. If drug-induced depression's severe, you may ask the doctor to consider switching the patient to another drug. In any case, be familiar with the drugs that have this side effect by studying the list on page 102.

Try to discover the cause of a patient's depression, in case it's something physical you can correct. However, don't waste precious time trying to analyze his problem. Do what you can to offer emotional support while you continue assessing his physical condition. If his depression seems severe or prolonged, take steps to refer him immediately. Don't risk a possible suicide attempt.

Recognizing depression

Learn to recognize the physical and emotional signs of depression. Watch for:
• erratic sleep patterns, especially early-morning insomnia
• apathy, including lack of interest in appearance
• appetite loss
• complaints of headache, fatigue, or reduced sex drive
• profound sadness, with crying spells
• hostility toward self and others
• irritability, particularly toward those who are energetic or lively
• anxiety or despair, with strongly expressed fears of death.

If your patient shows any of these signs, document what you observe in your notes. Then report his depression to the doctor for further evaluation.

How to help

While you're waiting for a more extensive assessment of your patient's condition, do your best to relieve his stress. Use the following guidelines to plan his care.
• First, accept the patient as he is. Don't reject him by saying things like "What's the matter with you?" or "Things aren't really that bad." Such remarks imply he has no right to feel depressed. Instead, try some of the conversational tips listed on page 93. Be friendly, but matter-of-fact. Don't act too sympathetic, or you'll encourage clinging behavior.
• Reinforce your patient's positive behavior by praising the things he does well. Encourage him to continue doing things for himself.
• Guide his decision-making. His depression may prevent him from making decisions. Offer positive suggestions. Don't increase his stress by saying: "Mr. Carson, when are you going to get up and get some exercise?" Instead, say: "I'll be back in 5 minutes, so we can walk down the hall."
• Promote good nutrition and adequate fluid intake. Encourage him to eat by giving him small meals, snacks, and appetizing finger foods. Ask his family to bring his favorite foods from home. Make sure he gets enough fluids and bulk to prevent possible elimination problems.
• Provide an environment that he can cope with easily. Do your best to minimize noise and confusion.
• Encourage your patient to talk about his feelings. Since you can't be with him every minute, ask him to write down his feelings throughout the day so you can discuss them later.
• Promote natural sleep with back rubs, soothing conversation, or a warm bath. Avoid using medications to induce sleep.

The road back

By maintaining a calm, positive manner, you may succeed in easing the depressed patient's stress and lifting his spirits. However, don't consider yourself a failure if you can't help him. His depression may be so severe that he'll require psychiatric help. Never feel you have to succeed with every depressed patient; just do the best you can. Relieving even a little of his stress may help more than you realize.

"Unchecked depression is dangerous. It can cause a patient's stress level to become so intolerable that he may attempt suicide as a way to escape."

The threatened suicide

For example, suppose you're talking to a woman who's just lost her husband and only child in a house fire. Surely you understand how stunned she is by the tragedy, but how do you react when she tells you, "I wish I'd been killed in the fire, too. Everything I have has been taken from me." Do you think, "She doesn't really mean that. She's just overwhelmed by this tragedy," or "That feeling will pass once she works out her grief "?

Don't disregard her remarks. They suggest she thinks the pain's unbearable. In most cases, suicidal patients are torn between conflicting wishes: wanting to live and wanting to die. Take any plea for help seriously.

The past attempt

Consider a patient recently diagnosed with diabetes. When you're teaching him about his disease, he says: "I'll never get used to this." So you ask him how he's coped with big problems in the past. And he tells you, "Well, when my girlfriend left me, I overdosed." How do you react? Do you think: "I suppose he thought she'd come back to him. But that's all over now. He won't try that again"?

Don't minimize his disclosure. This patient's tried suicide before as a coping mechanism. He could use it again. If his history shows that any members of his family have committed suicide, stay alert. He may consider it, too, especially if he has unresolved guilt feelings about them.

The reckless patient

Suppose you're admitting a patient to the E.D. and you ask him when he had his last tetanus shot. He tells you he was given one just 4 days earlier. When you inquire about it, you learn that he's suffered several injuries recently. Do you think, "He's really accident prone" or "He's certainly had a lot of bad luck lately"?

Don't disregard this important clue. Many suicidal patients seem to invite serious accidents by behaving recklessly. Always suspect any self-destructive tendencies as potentially suicidal.

The depressed patient

Consider the tennis pro who's just had a leg amputated. Not

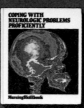

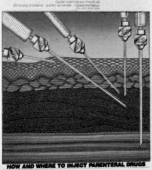

Choose one of these important books as your introductory volume when you join the NURSING SKILLBOOK series...the most comprehensive reference series ever published for nurses.

• Using Crisis Intervention Wisely • Coping With Neurologic Problems Proficiently • Managing Diabetics Properly • Helping Cancer Patients Effectively • Documenting Patient Care Responsibly • Monitoring Fluid and Electrolytes Precisely • Giving Cardiovascular Drugs Safely • Assessing Vital Functions Accurately • Nursing Critically Ill Patients Confidently • Giving Emergency Care Competently • Reading EKGs Correctly • Combatting Cardiovascular Diseases Skillfully • Dealing with Death and Dying

FACTS AND FABLES ABOUT SUICIDE

Don't let popular misconceptions about suicide cloud your understanding. Here's a chart to help you separate fact from fable. Read it carefully. Then, use the information to guide your patient's family. Remember, unless they perceive the patient's situation realistically, he'll be missing an important source of support.

FABLE	FACT
"People who talk about suicide don't commit suicide."	Eight out of ten people who commit suicide have given definite warnings of their intentions. Almost no one commits suicide without first letting others know how he feels.
"You can't stop a suicidal person. He's fully intent on dying."	Most suicidal people can't decide whether to live or die. Neither wish is necessarily stronger. For suicide to happen, three things must coincide: the will to die, the means to kill, and the energy to carry out the plan.
"Once a person's suicidal, he's suicidal forever."	People who want to kill themselves are only suicidal for a limited time. If they're saved from feelings of self-destruction, they can go on to lead normal lives.
"Improvement after severe depression means that the suicidal risk is over."	Most suicides occur within about 3 months after the beginning of "improvement," when the individual has the energy to carry out suicidal intentions.
"Suicide strikes the rich and the poor more than the middle class."	Suicide is neither the rich man's disease nor the poor man's cure. Suicide is represented proportionately among all levels of society.
"Suicide is an inherited trait."	Suicide does not run in families. It is an individual matter and can be prevented. However, suicide by a close family member increases the risk for others, especially on the birthday or anniversary of the relative's death.
"People usually commit suicide by taking an overdose of drugs."	Gunshot wounds are the leading cause of death among suicide victims.
"If a patient has attempted suicide, he won't do it again."	Over 50% of those who commit suicide have previously attempted to do so.
"Surgery or childbirth has no effect on whether a patient will commit suicide."	Incidence of suicide rises whenever a patient's body image is severely threatened.
"Terminally ill patients are the ones most likely to commit suicide."	Terminally ill patients commit suicide less commonly than those with chronic illness. Persons over 60 years of age are most likely to commit suicide.
"All suicidal patients are psychotic."	Although the suicidal person is extremely depressed, he's not necessarily psychotic, just unable to see an alternative solution to his problems. For the psychotic patient, risk of suicide greatly increases.

only has he lost his leg, but he's lost his livelihood as well. Now you notice he's becoming increasingly sullen, disoriented, and depressed. Do you think, "He'll pull through this, just give him time," or "It's not *that* bleak. Today an artificial limb is almost like the real thing"?

Don't minimize his trauma. He faces the dual challenge of adjusting to a changed body image and finding a new profession. He'll surely have trouble coping. Learn to recognize depression before it threatens the patient's life. Watch for:

• changes in sleeping habits (especially early morning insomnia)
• changes in eating habits
• changes in activity patterns
• difficulty communicating (especially maintaining eye contact)
• unusually slow or faltering thought and speech
• indications of multiple-system illnesses
• abnormally long recovery time
• all-consuming interest in his own problems.

The personality change
Suppose the behavior of one of your patients changes dramatically. Mr. Turner, who's slowly recovering from a prostatectomy, is a quiet man. Most of the time, he seems deep in thought. Then overnight, he becomes talkative, expressive, confident, almost a different person. Do you think, "He's finally snapped out of his postop depression," or "He's getting better. Now I can stop worrying about him"?

Don't misread his behavior change. Drastic shifts in personality can indicate the patient's decided to attempt suicide and may already have a plan worked out. Usually the change begins with a transition period, when the patient makes resolutions and adopts a new routine. Perhaps he'll say: "I'm going to get my life organized." You may think his condition's improved. But don't be caught off-guard. In this period, more than any other, the patient's got the energy to attempt suicide. And remember, such changes aren't necessarily one-time occurrences. Some patients' moods seesaw dramatically. For example, a friendly patient may suddenly become hostile, then friendly, then hostile again later.

The distant patient

Consider the patient who seems cut off from those around her. First you discover she's been giving all her flowers to her roommate. Then you notice she's thrown out all her get-well cards from family and friends. Do you think: "She just needs time to herself. After a while she'll welcome her family's support"?

Don't overlook this clue. The patient's preparing for death. This danger sign's the hardest to detect because the patient's calmly predisposed toward suicide and may not show any abnormal behavior.

What if a patient in your care shows one of these danger signs? Perhaps you want to know: "Is he really in crisis? What should I say to him? How can I help him most?" Read on.

Taking threats seriously

First, accept the probability your patient's suicidal. Identify the danger signs. If the patient's told you, "I'm going to blow my brains out," his distress is obvious. But even if he only hints at suicide, take him seriously. Don't act shocked, or say, "Come on, you don't mean that." Instead say something like, "Things must really be rough for you." If you can, take him to a private area immediately so you can discuss it further.

Find out how he perceives the situation. Ask him what he thinks the problem is. He may give you a precise answer: "I can't live without my wife." Or he may be vague: "It's just everything." If he can't identify his problem, try to work through his nameless fear by focusing on his problem. Ask him, "When did you begin to feel this way?" "What was happening then that might have caused it?" Encourage him to talk. Summarize what he's told you. For example, you might say, "You seem to be telling me your separation's at the bottom of this."

Find out how he's coping. Ask him, "How did you feel when you learned your wife left you?" "What did you do then?" "Did it help?" Then ask him if he's ever thought of suicide. Don't worry that discussing suicide will increase the possibility that he'll attempt it; the opposite is true. Talking about his problems can be therapeutic and may delay an attempt. Ask him if he thinks suicide's his only option. He may

AFTER THE SUICIDE ATTEMPT

How do you manage the patient who's been hospitalized after a suicide attempt? If you think he may try again, ask yourself: "What can I do to prevent it?"

Consider Jean Ross, 19, who slashed her wrists after an argument with her boyfriend. After receiving prompt emergency care, she arrives at your unit. How do you begin assessing her condition? First, introduce yourself and try to establish a rapport. She'll need all the support you can give. In conversation, don't dwell on the physical part of her suicide attempt. Instead, focus on her emotions. Help her recall the event by asking: "What led up to it?" "Who was there?" "What was said?" "When did you decide to slash your wrists?" "What effect did it have?" "Was it worth it?" "How do you feel about it now?" "Would you ever try it again?"

Helping the patient
Is the patient still in severe stress? If so, he may try again to kill himself.

Intervene immediately by following these guidelines:
• Don't minimize the attempt or its significance. Be honest with the patient. Discuss his situation. When you make a referral, explain the value of long-term treatment.
• Help relieve his stress. How, specifically, can you do this? If he's in a semiprivate room, be sure his roommate's compatible. If he smokes, let him. If he likes watching TV or listening to the radio, make sure he can.
• Don't do anything that he might interpret as punishment. Make sure any physical restraints are for his protection and *not* just for

your convenience.
• Help the patient set goals to relieve the unbearable stress that precipitated his suicide attempt. But be careful. Don't solve his problems *for* him.
• Help rebuild his self-respect. If his condition permits, encourage him to participate in his care.
• Maintain good nutrition. If he won't eat three well-balanced meals a day, give him some nutritious snacks instead. Chances are, you'll find he eats more if you give him finger food, like sandwiches, chicken, and fruit.
• Don't make careless remarks, especially around the semi-comatose patient. They may be overheard by the patient, other nurses, or the family, and cause unnecessary embarrassment.
• Don't leave your patient alone. Never let him leave your floor without an attendant. Encourage family members to keep him company. Many hospitals hire people especially to stay with suicidal patients.
• Protect the patient. Remove any potentially lethal articles from his room. Watch what visitors bring him.
• Try to treat your patient as you would any other. If you pity him, he'll resent it. If you're too accommodating, he may feel he doesn't deserve the attention. If you act insecure or defensive when you're with him, he probably won't trust your judgment.

Dealing with the family
Most people respond to a loved one's suicide attempt by trying to forget it. Usually, the patient's family and friends avoid discussing it with him because they don't know what to say. The attempt may have either scared,

embarrassed, or puzzled them. Perhaps they feel guilty because they'd failed to detect their loved one's crisis. When they do discuss it, they do so awkwardly, which only compounds the patient's stress.

Teach the family about your patient's condition. Make sure they understand that his release from the hospital doesn't mean his problems are over. When he leaves, he'll need someone he can trust, as well as someone to accept and care for him. Make sure he has that support. If you don't, his life's still in danger.

Dealing with your feelings
How do you feel about suicide? Do you see it as a sign of character weakness? Or do you think the suicidal patient's trapped in circumstances beyond his control? Don't let either view intrude on the quality of your care.

If you see suicide as a character weakness, your words and actions may show impatience with, and perhaps disdain for, the patient. You may also focus on his physical problems and ignore his emotional ones. Guard against both reactions. Try to be as understanding as possible.

Viewing suicide as an emotional illness may make you try to resolve the patient's distress yourself. But that's neither your job nor within your capabilities. Instead, direct him to professional help.

Suppose a patient in your care attempts suicide. Don't feel guilty for not recognizing the danger signs. Placing blame on yourself or the patient is never constructive. Spend your energies on positive actions.

"Don't assume suicide's the act of a psychotic. A person may commit suicide because he fears a long, painful illness; he doesn't want to burden his family; or he's lost a loved one."

Is a drug causing your patient's depression?

When investigating the source of your patient's depression, don't overlook the possibility that his medication may be responsible. Here's a list of drugs whose side effects include depression:

- anorexiants
- asparaginase (Elspar)
- baclofen (Lioresal)
- barbiturates
- carisoprodol (Soma)
- chloramphenicol (Chloromycetin)
- clonidine (Catapres)
- dantrolene sodium (Dantrium)
- diazepam (Valium)
- diethylstilbesterol (DES)
- estrogen-containing products
- gentamicin (Garamycin)
- hydralazine (Apresoline)
- indomethacin (Indocin)
- methyldopa (Aldomet)
- pentazocine (Talwin)
- phenytoin (Dilantin)
- propranolol (Inderal)
- guanethidine (Ismelin)
- reserpine (Serpasil)
- sulfonamides
- tamoxifen (Nolvadex)
- trimethobenzamide (Tigan)
- tybamate

believe he has no alternative. Has he planned how he'll kill himself? Is that plan realistic? If it is, consider him an exceptionally high-risk patient, one who not only has a plan but a means to carry it out.

Keep your assessment brief. Don't spend precious time trying to determine how soon a patient may attempt suicide. If you think he's suicidal, get help immediately. He needs special counseling that you're not able to give. Your greatest service to him is recognizing his need for outside help and getting it.

Tell the patient you're referring him. He may react strongly with anger, hopelessness, fear, guilt, or anxiety. How should you respond? For example, what if he thinks you're abandoning him? Assure him of your continued concern by saying something like, "I'm calling someone who can help you more than I can. I want to do what's best for you." How will he react to this news? For some examples of possible reaction to referral, see page 36.

Before you leave the patient, arrange for an aide or a family member to stay with him. Then document exactly what he's told you, as well as what you've observed.

The referral art: You and other health professionals

Before you call the doctor, be prepared to explain why you think the patient's suicidal, but never hesitate to make a referral for fear you're overreacting. Even if your assessment seem inconclusive, respect your gut feelings. Well-meaning overreaction can't kill your patient. Your failure to act can.

What if the patient's doctor refuses to allow a referral? He may tell you the patient's had bouts with depression all his life. Or he may want to handle the problem himself. Or, like many people, he could be reluctant to face the patient's suicidal tendencies. If he won't help, check your hospital's written policy. Perhaps you can go directly to a psychiatric nurse practitioner or the social service department. However, if all avenues are closed to you, tell your supervisor how you feel. And document your observations in your notes. Keep the other nurses in your unit informed about the patient as well.

If you're in a specialty unit and observe any of suicide's danger signs just before you transfer a patient to a regular unit, alert his new nurses to the danger signs. Ultimately, that intervention may later save time and confirm doubts in critical situations.

The referral art: You and the patient

Usually, outside help isn't immediately available. What do you do to protect your patient while you're waiting? Try to make a pact with him. Say: "Promise me you won't do anything to hurt yourself before we talk again. Call me when you need me." This sort of agreement may keep the suicidal patient from acting impulsively. Your pact makes him responsible to you as well as himself. But hold up your end of the bargain. Make yourself available.

Take these additional precautions:

• Relieve his immediate stress. For example, if he fears surgery or dislikes therapy, ask the doctor to consider delaying. If your patient can't get along with his roommate, arrange to move him.

• Try to remove any potentially lethal items, like scissors, nail files, belts, or toxic fluids, from his room.

• Examine anything a patient's visitors bring him. They may unwittingly supply him with other potentially lethal items.

• Does he say you're the only one he can talk to? Don't encourage these feelings. Such attitudes will make referral very difficult.

• Don't rush the referral process. Explain what you must do, then ease the patient into it. Instead of transferring him immediately to a psychiatric unit, ask the psychologist or social worker to come to him.

• Stay with the patient as much as possible. If you can't be there, have a member of his family, a trusted friend, or a hospital aide keep him company. Never leave a high-risk patient alone, even for a moment.

The real tragedy

Don't expect to avert a tragedy every time you have a suicidal patient to deal with. Even the most skilled professional must be ready to accept defeat sometimes. But you can help by recognizing suicide's danger signs early and making a swift referral. Most of us will never know the depths of hopelessness

A plea for help

Suppose you answer a phone call from someone who says, "I can't stand being alone any more. I'm going to kill myself. Don't try to stop me—my mind's made up." What do you say?

If you're the least bit uncertain, review the following guidelines. Remember, the person who's calling wants and needs your help. Deal with him calmly. Speak slowly and clearly.

• First, try to find out how the caller plans to kill himself and if he has those means available.

• Next, find out where he is and send help immediately. Don't wait until he hangs up. Have someone call the police or rescue squad. Try to keep him on the phone.

• Encourage him to tell you what's bothering him. Try to change his mind about suicide by urging him to explore other options. For example, say: "What other ways can you cope with this problem?"

• Don't scold or argue. Keep your tone sympathetic and supportive.

Important: If he's already taken pills, find out what kind and how many. Don't be fooled if he says, "I don't remember." If he can talk, he's capable of recalling what he took.

and despair that drive a person to kill himself. But as tragic as suicide is, an even greater tragedy is when someone tells us he's going to kill himself—and no one listens.

Where to refer the patient and his family

When a suicidal patient is released from the hospital, be sure to give him and his family the phone number of your local Crisis Intervention Hotline. For more information about suicide prevention, write to the following organizations:

- American Association of Suicidology, 1200 Moursund Rd., Houston, Tex. 77025
- International Association for Suicide Prevention, 2521 W. Pico Blvd., Los Angeles, Calif. 90006.

Helping the victims of child abuse

NURSING SKILLBOOK STAFF IN CONSULTATION
WITH DOROTHY A. HYDE, RN, MS, CPNA

YOU MIGHT SAY AN ABUSED CHILD is a "silent screamer."
What other patient would sit quietly through an examination
and not tell you how desperately he needs your help? "Hearing" his cry is up to you.

If you work in an emergency department, doctor's office,
school nurse's office, or in patients' homes, you may see an
abused child today. Will you recognize his plight? Will you
know what injuries point to child abuse? What accident stories
don't sound plausible?

Suppose you do suspect child abuse. You're legally obliged
to report it. But do you have the courage to stand alone behind
your report if no one else wants to get involved?

In this chapter, I'll discuss how to recognize and help the
abused child. And I'll tell you how to cope with your own
outraged feelings, which'll probably get in your way. Caring
for a brutalized child will hurt and anger you. Be prepared
to accept this. But take comfort in knowing you can prevent
further abuse by prompt intervention.

Watch for telltale signs
How can you tell for sure when a child's been abused? You

can't always, because abuse injuries can resemble those caused by accident. Know what to look for when you make your initial assessment. Suspect child abuse anytime a child has the following:

• an injury for which there's no explanation or an implausible explanation
• a large number of healed or partially healed injuries
• a large bone fracture (in a child under one year)
• an unusual number of accidents.

Also suspect child abuse if the child's been in your E.D. many times or if your hospital's a long way from the child's home. An abusive parent may switch from one emergency department to another to avoid suspicion.

Was it really an accident?

Now, let's expand on these guidelines so you know exactly what to look for. As soon as you've assessed the child's injuries and provided prompt emergency care, find out as much as you can about the accident.

Talk to the parents. Do you detect inconsistencies in their stories? Or a vagueness about details? Check it out. Discuss the accident again when the doctor's present.

Suppose the parents can't tell you exactly what happened. Stay alert, especially if they're quick to blame a babysitter or neighbor for the accident. Unless the injuries seem life-threatening, most parents try to learn accident details before they come to the hospital.

Does the child *look* like he just had an accident? Are his clothes dirty? His face smudged? His hair tousled? Or is he freshly scrubbed with every hair in place? Be suspicious. The child who just fell out of a tree and broke his arm won't look spotless. Perhaps an abusive parent caused his injury.

Think about the explanation you've been given for the accident. How plausible is it? For example, can a 3-week-old baby roll off the bed? Of course not. Always question an illogical explanation for an injury, but don't assume it's a lie. Without close supervision, some children will try anything.

Consider the injuries

Do the injuries fit the accident? Use your common sense. Suppose a child steps into a tub that he's accidentally filled with scalding water. Will he burn both feet? Chances are, he

"Not all abusive parents actually batter their children. Some may vent their frustrations on the child's favorite toys instead."

Dealing with potential child abusers

How can you recognize a potential child abuser? What can you do to avert abuse before it happens?

Prevention begins in the maternity unit. After birth, observe the mother's interaction with her baby. Does she examine and cuddle him affectionately? Or does she avoid looking at him and talking about him?

What can you do to ease a new mother's stress?

• Tell her what to expect after she takes her baby home. Correct her misconceptions and help her develop realistic expectations.

• Discuss what disturbs her most about the baby. If she's concerned about the baby's physical care, suggest she come to a group class or give her the necessary instruction yourself.

• Never force a reluctant mother to hold her baby. Develop their relationship slowly. Let the mother see her baby for short periods. If she becomes distressed, take the baby away.

• Don't push breast-feeding on the unwilling mother. She may be reluctant to do it because of family pressure or fear of failure.

• Before discharge, provide new support systems and options for coping. Give the mother a list of agencies, child care centers, and telephone hot lines if she needs help. Make sure she knows who she can call at your hospital too.

won't. Like most of us, he'll put one foot in at a time, withdrawing immediately if the water's too hot.

If a child tips a pot of hot coffee on his hand, his burn will probably have a *splash* pattern. Be suspicious if it covers his hand like a mitten.

Consider the child's age when there's a bone fracture. In most cases, a child's bones remain very pliable until he's old enough to walk. A direct blow, not a fall, is more apt to cause a fracture.

If you see a subdural hematoma in a child of any age, ask the doctor to order long-bone X-rays to find fractures. Look for multiple fractures, especially tearing of the periosteum caused by the shearing action of having a limb forcibly twisted.

Assess the child's condition carefully. Pay particular attention to his abdomen and head. *Nursing tip:* To discover hard-to-see head bruises, walk your fingers across his scalp. Usually, a child will flinch when you touch a tender spot.

Look for these other signs of possible abuse:

• human bite marks
• fingernail indentations or scratches
• injury to oral mucosa or frontal dental ridge from having bottle forced in mouth
• old or new cigarette burns
• loop marks from belt beating
• soft tissue swelling, hematomas, or numerous healed lesions
• multiple or clustered bruises: on trunk or buttocks; in body hollows, particularly small of back; or resembling hand prints or pinch marks
• bald spots
• multiple fractures
• retinal hemorrhage from being shaken or cuffed about the head
• dislocations or wrenching injuries from jerking child
• burns that resemble socks on feet, or mittens on hands; burns with unusual patterns, for example, coil or grid marks. *Important:* Does the child have what looks like a scald burn? Examine it closely. Make sure it isn't scalded skin syndrome, a staphylococcus infection.

Watch those interactions

Note how the child and his parents act and interact. Do you sense something's wrong? For example, does the child flinch when you touch him or glance about nervously? Does he seem afraid of his parents or reluctant to return home?

Don't ignore what parents say to the child, particularly if he cries. Always suspect anyone who issues this threat to a whimpering child: "Just wait till I get you home!" Similarly, suspect the parent who remains completely indifferent to his child's distress.

Do one or both parents blame the child for his own injuries? For example, do they say: "He's always getting hurt. He obviously does it just to cause trouble." Ask them to explain. Say: "When was the last time he had an accident that required emergency treatment?" For other tips on what to say in cases of possible child abuse, see page 113.

Investigate behavior that suggests role reversal. For example, does a parent solicit adult protectiveness from the child by acting helpless? When unrealistic expectations like this aren't met, the parent may become angry and abusive.

Don't assume you can detect a child abuser easily. He may not fit the stereotype you envision. For example, he's not necessarily a teenage parent, a slum-dweller, or an alcoholic. He may be a business executive, a church leader, or doctor or nurse.

Consider this:

• A mother who repeatedly brings a healthy child to the clinic may be a potential abuser. Of course, this woman may just be overprotective or need reassurance that she's a good mother. But she may be trying to tell you she can't cope with parenthood. If so, you can stop a potential abuser before she gets started.

In one such case, a young mother brought her infant daughter to a clinic three times in one week, complaining that the child had diarrhea. The baby looked healthy and his stool specimen was normal.

When told that her baby was fine, the mother began to cry. A sympathetic nurse probed her reaction, and the mother finally blurted out, "If you don't keep her here, I'll kill her. All my friends are out having a good time, and I'm stuck in the house with this baby. I can't stand it." Then the nurse discovered the baby was illegitimate, the father had deserted his family, and the mother—only 18 years old—was on drugs. With the nurse's intervention the child was hospitalized and a social service agency was called in. That nurse may have

SEXUAL ABUSE: WHEN THE VICTIM'S A CHILD

Young girls aren't the only children who suffer sexual abuse.

Boys and girls of any age, even tiny infants, can be victims. The abuser may be a stranger, but most likely he's someone the child knows—one of his parents, another relative, an older child, or a family friend.

When a child complains she's been sexually abused, take her seriously. Never assume she's told her family, or that they'd believe her if she did tell them. Such news may so shock them that they choose to ignore it or even punish the child for "lying."

In some cases, the child may have been told that abuse is a way someone expresses affection, so she may not complain at all.

Learn to recognize sexual abuse, and take action against it. Remember, even the parent who knows what's going on may be reluctant to report it if the abuser's a family member.

Don't assume that sexual abuse is always accompanied by battering — sometimes it's not. But if a child has symptoms of V.D., consider sexual abuse the cause. Also, be suspicious when you see:
• other venereal infections; i.e., trichomonas, herpes, or monilia
• genital or rectal injuries
• bloody or painful urination or bowel movements.

Important: Report all cases of suspected sexual abuse to the police. Then follow the procedures for collecting evidence explained in Chapter 8.

What you can do
Suppose you're treating a 10-year-old girl and you suspect she's been sexually abused.

First, take the parents aside and inform them of your suspicions. Don't assume they're guilty. They may not have been involved. Offer your support, emphasizing your concern for the child. Ask them to tell you things about the child that'll help you speak to her on her own level; for example, ask what words she uses to describe various body parts. Then find out the following.
• What are the names of family members and frequent visitors?
• Who babysits for the child?
• What are the family sleeping arrangements?
• Does the child have behavioral problems, like excessive masturbation? When did they begin?
• Does she have any phobias? Is she fearful of any particular person or place? Does she have nightmares?

Interview the child
With this background information, you'll find it easier to communicate with the child. Use the suggestions on page 112 to establish rapport with her. Then ask questions like:
• Has anyone ever taken your panties off?
• Has anyone ever put his finger (or any other object) between your legs?
• Does anyone ever get in bed with you at night?

Without letting her see how upset you are, encourage her to talk about her feelings. Don't let her sense that you're horrified, or she may become frightened and ashamed.

Prepare the child for a pelvic exam
Don't focus exclusively on the pelvic area when you get

her ready for the exam. Complete these procedures first:
• Make a record of any bruises, abrasions, or other injuries.
• Look for signs of secretions in the mouth, pharynx, hair and skin.
• Check for pelvic hematomas with a rectoabdominal exam.

Because a pelvic exam's likely to be a new experience for your patient, take plenty of time to explain it to her and answer her questions. In some cases, the doctor will want to anesthetize the patient before the exam.

Remember, the prepubescent vagina is extremely sensitive. For that reason, the doctor won't use a cotton tip applicator or tongue blade to get specimens of secretions. Instead, he'll use a sterile plastic medicine dropper lubricated with sterile water. If the child is small, provide him with a nasal speculum or an infant-sized vaginoscope. Take care to lubricate the instruments with water and warm them to room temperature.

Important: Make sure girls who are past menarche are tested for pregnancy. Test all children who may have suffered sexual abuse for V.D.

Where to refer
In cases of child abuse, both the parents and child need counseling. The child will have fears and anxieties that may produce unusual behavior. Her parents need to know how to help her work through the trauma. Advise the parents not to punish or scold the child when she works through her emotions by masturbating or playing out the event with dolls.

"Boys and girls of any age, even tiny infants, can be sexually abused. The abuser may be a stranger, but most likely he's someone the child knows."

When an abused child is hospitalized

You're caring for two abused children, both age 10. Susie's a difficult patient. Because she's learned that causing trouble attracts attention, she quarrels with the other children and rebels against hospital rules.

Helen, on the other hand, is quiet and submissive. She's pathetically insecure and clings to any adult who passes by.

Despite the differences, you can help each child if you:
• Encourage her to express her feelings, both verbally and through play. But don't pry. If she clearly doesn't want to talk about what's happened, don't pursue the subject.
• Give her a sense of control by preparing her for discharge. If she's going to go to a foster home, tell her. Arrange for her to meet the foster parents while she's in the hospital, if possible.
• Channel her energy by involving her in her care. You might let her help on the unit; for example, straightening up the play room.
• Set limits and keep them consistent.

Don't overindulge Helen, even though she's pitiful. And don't withhold affection from Susie, even if she doesn't return it. Treat both children evenhandedly, with warmth and acceptance.

Also avoid:
• Indulging in "rescue" fantasies. Remember, you're limited in what you can do.
• Rejecting or ignoring parents. If possible, include them in the child's care.

When they visit, observe the family's behavior and encourage positive interactions.

averted a tragedy.

Remember, even when parents seem concerned and loving, a child isn't immune from abuse. Today's children are exposed to a variety of potential abusers: babysitters, a parent's live-in lover or occasional friend, extended-family members like uncles and grandparents, or even neighbors.

Talk to the child

At the first opportunity, talk to the child alone. Ask the parents to wait outside while you finish examining him.

Attempt to establish some rapport with him. If you find this difficult, show an interest in a toy he may be carrying or offer to draw some pictures with him.

Be gentle. Ask "What happened to you?" If he won't answer, don't persist or try to put words in his mouth. Instead, say "It's okay if you don't want to talk about it." Never expect a child to admit he's been mistreated, even when he's been badly beaten. Why? Because he may think such treatment is normal, if abuse is all he's ever known. Or he may feel great loyalty to his parents and fear that they'll desert him. He may be terrified that his parents will abuse him further if he tells you too much. Tragically, he may even think he deserves abuse because he's bad.

Suppose he does tell you his parents punished him for being naughty. Don't attempt to console him by saying "Well, sometimes parents hit harder than they mean to when they're upset." A statement like this indicates you think such abuse is okay. Instead, try to find out what stresses in the family led up to the violence. Say something like: "Tell me everything that happened just before you got punished."

Question the parents

Next, talk to the parents. Go to a room where you won't be disturbed, but make sure the child knows where you are. Have someone stay with him. Then do your best to make the parents comfortable, no matter what you suspect.

I realize this won't be easy. Depending on your feelings, you may find it impossible to talk to the parents calmly. If you can't, acknowledge those feelings and ask someone else to relieve you.

Don't bombard the parents with questions they'll interpret as accusatory. Instead, work up to the subject of their child

CONVERSATION

GENERAL GUIDELINES	WHEN SHE SAYS:	DON'T SAY:	SAY:
Don't encourage scape-goating.	"If my husband was home more, I could handle the kids."	"I know what you mean."	"Have you talked to him about it?"
Don't negate feelings.	"I can't stand this child another day."	"Come on, it can't be that bad."	"What about him annoys you most?"
Emphasize positive features.	"Why can't I be a good mother?"	"Tell me how your mother treated you."	"You can be. Showing concern is an important step."
Encourage the patient to introduce topics of conversation.	(Child says nothing.)	"Did you really fall down the steps?"	"What are you thinking about?"

gradually. For specific tips on how to manage this difficult interview, see the conversation chart above.

Whatever you do, don't give the impression that you're criticizing them, trying to impart your own values, or acting as their judge. Putting them on the defensive won't make them cooperate, and it may keep them from accepting help from other health-care professionals.

Do your best to be tolerant and understanding. Try to determine how realistically they perceive the child, how they cope with the stresses of parenting, and where they turn for support. As you talk, attempt to get answers to the following questions:

• "What do you do when he cries too much? If that doesn't work, what do you do?"

• "Does the child sleep well? What do you do when he doesn't sleep?"

• "How do you discipline him?"

• "How do you feel after you've disciplined the child?"

• "Are you ever angry because the child takes up so much of your time?"

• "Does he take up more time than your other children, or

The neglected child

Not all abused children are battered. Some suffer just as cruelly from another type of abuse — parental neglect, either willful or unintentional.

What is neglect? Sometimes it's simply a lack of adequate food, clothing, and shelter. But it can also be inadequate love, concern, and attention.

Neglect can take many forms. In some cases, a parent may neglect a child by simply "forgetting" about him; for example, leaving him behind at a bus terminal after rounding up the other children. In other cases, a parent may sedate a rejected child to keep him quiet; belittle him until he's convinced he's worthless; or hurt him by physically abusing his pet or favorite toy.

How can you spot a neglected child? Watch for:
• signs of malnutrition, including wasting of subcutaneous tissue, abdominal distention, thinness, pallor, dull eyes, sore gums
• inadequate clothing in cold weather
• apathy or hyperexcitability
• behavior problems
• emotional or developmental immaturity
• parasitic infections
• depression, neurosis, or psychosomatic illness
• parental role-playing among siblings. When all the children in a family are neglected, older children will sometimes "mother" the younger ones.

A neglected child needs help as much as one who's been beaten. Notify your community's child protection service.

require more disciplining?   If he does, why do you think he does?"
• "Do you think he misbehaves on purpose?"
• "Who do you usually talk to when your child upsets you? Is that person available now?"
• "Was this child planned?" (Don't assume that every woman who wanted an abortion, or could have gotten one, did so.)
• "Did both of you want this child?"

As you discuss things, try to determine what the situation is at home. Do one or both of the parents seem unduly distressed? Perhaps they're facing other stresses they can't cope with: for example, a job loss, loneliness, illness, or alcoholism.

Watch for clues that the child reminds them of a relative or former spouse they dislike. Then explore this possibility with gentle questions. For example, say: "It must be really upsetting for you when he acts like his father. What goes through your mind then?" Or say: "In what ways is she like your mother? Do those characteristics irritate you?"

Take action

If the answers to your questions indicate abuse, take action immediately. Don't wait to see if the child has another "accident." He may not survive the next one. Your prompt intervention at this point is crucial. You'll also be helping the parents, who may be abusing their child because of stresses they can't cope with.

First, tell the doctor about your suspicions. He may want to hospitalize the child for observation and tests, if he feels it's justified. Then explain to the parents what you've done and indicate that you want to help. In some cases, they may be relieved that someone recognizes the problems and wants to intervene. In other cases, they may object strenuously and try to take the child home. If that happens, the doctor may have to get an order from the police or other legal authorities to retain the child.

Make sure the parents know what to expect. Explain that a referral doesn't mean their child will be taken away from them or that they'll have to go through a court hearing. Try to consider their feelings. They're probably more upset than you are. Don't cope with your own stress by adding to theirs.

Next, report your suspicions to the proper agency by phone and then by written report. This agency may be the police,

"Not all abused children are battered. Some suffer just as cruelly from another type of abuse—parental neglect."

CHILD ABUSE: A CASE HISTORY

You're on duty in the E.D. when Mrs. Collins comes in with her 2-month-old son Jeff. She tells you that "I was driving him to the babysitter's when my car was hit by a truck. Jeff was lying on the front seat and was thrown to the floor. He hit the dashboard when he fell. Later on, his knee swelled up and I decided to have a doctor look at it."

What's happened to Jeff?

Because of the nature of the accident, you look closely at Jeff for head and neck injuries. You're surprised to find none, but you do notice some bruises on his left arm that look several weeks old. When you ask Mrs. Collins how he got them, she turns away and says tersely, "Jeff bruises easily."

Although the injury to the knee looks painful, Jeff lies quietly while you examine him. But when you comment on his listlessness, Mrs. Collins shrugs it off: "It's over 2 hours past his bedtime."

What should you think? Consider this evidence:
• A sore knee is the only injury Jeff allegedly sustained in the accident, although his mother says he was thrown violently from the car seat.
• His bruised arm shows that he's been hurt before. Mrs. Collins seems uncomfortable when you ask about it. She deliberately evades your questions and won't tell you exactly what happened.
• Jeff's manner is subdued, even groggy, despite obvious pain. In fact, he acts like he's been drugged.

Mrs. Collins' story just doesn't add up. You suspect Jeff's been abused.

What do you do next?

Tell the doctor what you suspect and ask him to order a total body X-ray. If he resists your request, talk directly to the radiologist; he can do it on his own authority. Don't hesitate to speak up. Remember, Jeff's life may be at stake.

Meanwhile, get an order for a blood coagulation profile to see whether Jeff bruises as easily as his mother says. Because you suspect drug abuse, get orders for toxicology studies of his blood and urine, too. Although you won't have all the results immediately, they may be important for future legal action. And don't forget to report suspected abuse to the appropriate child protection agency.

What Jeff's X-rays show

Jeff's X-ray on the opposite page reveals three fractures: a very recent chip fracture of the right knee, a spiral fracture of the shaft of the left ulna and radius (corresponding to the bruises you noticed), and a nearly-healed left clavicle fracture (as evidenced by callus formation). This X-ray strongly suggests that Jeff's been battered. Here's how you know:
• A chip fracture results from jerking a limb with such force that the ligaments are ripped away from the bone, carrying bits of the bone with them. A blow to the joint can't cause this type of break. Therefore, Mrs. Collins' story doesn't conform to the facts.
• A spiral fracture is caused by a twisting injury. In a baby, it nearly always points to abuse.
• Multiple fractures in different stages of healing, especially in such a young child, suggest a history of abuse.

How can you help Mrs. Collins?

Talk to her, following the guidelines on page 113. Don't assume that she hurt Jeff; someone else could be abusing him. But even if she is responsible, don't conclude she doesn't love him. She's probably worried about him and ashamed at her loss of control.

Do your best to gain her confidence. Avoid judgmental gestures. Don't:
• Walk in front of her or turn your back.
• Direct your questions away from her.
• Avoid eye contact.
• Ignore her or her comments.
• Stand over her when she's sitting.

Confronting Mrs. Collins with the facts

When you tell Mrs. Collins what the X-rays show, she seems actually relieved. Now that the problem's out in the open, she can talk to you about her fears. She explains that she loses her temper when Jeff cries, and gets "too rough" with him. Sometimes she gives him a little alcohol to quiet him down.

Jeff's being hospitalized for his injuries, but give his mother a chance to see him before she goes. She seems to feel better after telling him she's sorry, even though he's too young to understand.

Don't forget to give her the address and phone number of a local group like Child Abuse Prevention Effort and encourage her to call. Remind her, too, that someone from the Child Protection Service will be contacting her.

Feel positive about your actions. Remember, by helping her, you're also helping Jeff.

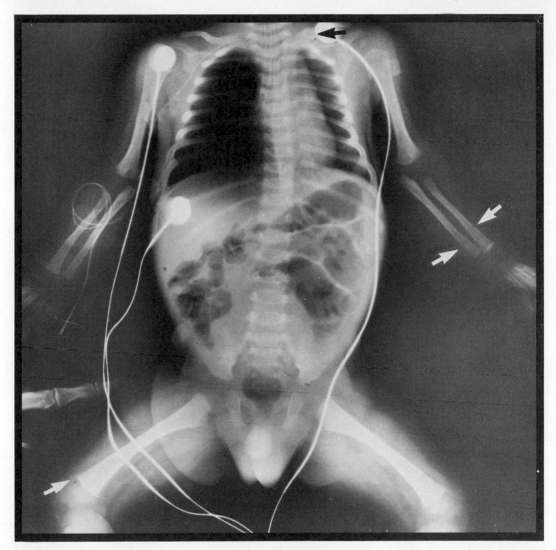

Reading Jeff's X-ray

This total body X-ray shows
many signs of child abuse. Study
it carefully, using the case
history on the opposite page to
guide you. First, examine the
right knee on the X-ray. If
you compare it to the left one,
you'll notice a chip separated
from the widest part of the
femur, or epiphysis. No evidence of a hematoma is visible,
because the injury just occurred.

Next, study the area of old
bruises on Jeff's left arm. Compare the ulna and radius with
the same bones on the opposite
arm. Notice the bones on the
right arm show clear, smooth
outlines. The left ones do not.
This periosteal elevation on
the left arm is caused by fibrin
collection around the broken

bones.

Finally, study the area indicated by the arrow near Jeff's
clavicle. Notice the formation of
calcium deposits in this area.
Within 10 days after a fracture,
these deposits begin to fill
the fibrin network.

In Jeff's case, the findings on
this particular X-ray were
conclusive evidence of child
abuse.

the district attorney's office, a child-protective service, or a social service group. Keep a list of agencies. If you don't know which one to report to in your community, call either the police or the local government social service bureau. Either one will tell you which agency to contact.

Expect them to ask you what *you* would recommend in the situation. For example, they may say: "Do you think this child's life will be in jeopardy if he returns home?" Don't be forced into making this decision. Instead, tell them what you've observed and ask them to come to the hospital. Say: "This decision should be made by someone with more experience than I have."

In your written report, *carefully* document the physical evidence of abuse. Describe exactly how parents and child interact. But take care what you write. Don't let your anger show through your words. All 50 states (and the District of Columbia) provide immunity to professionals who report abuse, or suspected abuse, in honesty and good faith. Indeed, many state laws make your *failure* to report it a crime. Here are some other helpful tips:

• Flag or list the names of children who are repeatedly brought to the hospital with injuries. Make sure the notes on the chart include what the parents said, how they reacted, and how they explained the accident.

• Provide other hospitals in the area with the names on file. Urge them to do the same with their files. Then take the time to check with other hospitals when you have a case you question. Perhaps the ward secretary can help you.

Never forget, child abuse can occur in any segment of our society. To combat it, we must stay alert for its danger signs and move quickly to report it. The abused child may never tell you he's mistreated, but he's crying for your help. Don't ignore him. You may be the only one who hears.

Where to refer the patient and his family
When you suspect unbearable stress may cause someone to abuse or neglect a child, provide a list of the following:
• **Childline Hotline. Phone: 717-783-8744**
• **Child Abuse Listening Mediation. Phone: 805-963-1115**
• **Child Abuse Prevention Effort. Phone: 215-831-8877**
• **National Committee for Prevention of Child Abuse, 111 East Walker Dr., Suite 510, Chicago, Ill. 60607.**

8

Comforting and caring for the rape victim

BY CARMEN GERMAINE WARNER, RN, PHN

RAPE. MORE SO THAN MOST situational crises, this violent act engulfs its victim in fear—of physical mutilation, psychologic trauma, and death. In most cases, the rape victim must struggle with unwarranted feelings of shame, guilt, and embarrassment. Her overwhelming agony may even keep her from seeking emergency care, or from reporting the crime.

But when you do see a rape victim in the hospital or clinic, how can you help her? Can you deal effectively with her feelings, as well as your own? Do you know what to say? How to meet her most pressing needs? Suppose she can't decide what to do about the rape: for example, whether or not to tell her family. How can you help her think things through without making decisions for her?

If you're uncertain, you need to read this chapter. In it, I'll tell you how to:

• Establish immediate rapport with the victim and her family (if they're present).

• Determine her special needs.

• Reduce her anxiety and restore her self-esteem.

• Prepare her for an examination and collection of evidence.

• Assist her with decisions, if necessary.

When a rape victim's hospitalized

What special care should you give a rape victim who's been admitted for multiple injuries?

• Treat her physical injuries, but never forget she's also a rape victim. Do your best to strengthen her balancing factors.

• If she's unconscious, have someone stay with her until she awakens. Talk to her normally, taking care what you say. Remember, she may later recall every word.

• Gather specimens and clothing for the police immediately. Don't risk losing essential evidence by delaying this important task.

• Watch for symptoms of vaginal infection like itching or discharge and report them to the doctor.

Keep in mind that a rape victim may experience disturbing flashbacks of the attack. Sometimes they're triggered by nursing procedures like perineal care or insertion of a Foley catheter. While she may become agitated during flashbacks, don't assume she'll always act that way. She may just lie quietly with a vacant stare, showing signs of shallow breathing, rigidity, and confusion.

Show her you accept her, no matter how she's coping. Encourage her to talk and give her as much control over her own care as possible. Continue your support until she's discharged.

Is the rape victim in crisis?

Face your feelings squarely. Caring for the rape victim immediately after the event won't be easy, no matter how well you're prepared. But do your best. She'll need your understanding to relieve her profound distress and possibly prevent crisis.

As you begin your assessment, take care what you say and do. Don't intensify a crisis in your patient. Try to appear calm, but don't act so casual that you appear indifferent. Let your patient know that you share her horror of what's happened—that you won't brush it off as "just another emergency."

Encourage her to talk about it. But be prepared to listen, no matter how difficult that may be for you. Take what she says seriously, even if her story has inconsistencies. A rape victim may be so disoriented that her first account of the assault doesn't make sense.

Don't criticize her—or let anyone else criticize her—for the way she acts and talks. The shock of rape may cause her to behave unusually. At various times during your initial assessment and the doctor's examination, you can expect some or all of these shock-related signs:

• inconsistencies in her story
• incoherent speech
• confusion about numbers
• inability to determine time intervals
• crying, with periods of uncontrollable sobbing
• restlessness or tenseness
• inappropriate smiling or laughing
• extreme anger, accompanied by wishes for revenge.

You may even see an occasional patient who hides her extreme stress under an unusually calm, composed exterior. When you do, watch her closely. No matter how calmly she relates the details of her assault, never let anyone refuse to take her seriously. Instead, try to estimate her internal stress level; it may be greater than that of the patient who shows her distress.

Be aware of your own feelings during this stressful time. Caring for a rape victim will probably arouse fears that you or someone you love might be raped someday. Watch how you cope with these fears. For example, how do you try to convince yourself it can't happen to you? Do you think "She asked for it," or "I don't believe half these stories"?

"Rape is a violent crime. The victim may suffer multiple physical injuries, as well as psychologic ones."

The male rape victim

Is the rape victim a man? Make sure he gets the same gentle consideration you'd give a woman who's been sexually attacked. Remember, he suffers the same feelings of shame, fear, guilt, and embarrassment that she does. Don't add to his humiliation by asserting that a man can't be raped. And never assume that he's somehow less masculine or even homosexual because of it.

Be especially alert for:
• Bleeding from rectal tears.
• Multiple injuries, both external and internal, from a severe beating. Considerable violence usually accompanies male rape because the physical strength of rapist and victim is likely to be comparable. And, in some cases, the male victim may have been gang raped.
• Signs of drug or alcohol intoxication. The victim may have been drugged or encouraged to drink excessively before the attack.

Another important reminder: The male rape victim needs the same prophylactic treatment for venereal disease as the female victim.

If you do, keep these thoughts to yourself. Never express them where your patient can hear you. You'll destroy whatever confidence she had in you and replace it with a wall of distrust. Instead, talk these feelings over later with your co-workers or a rape counselor.

Knowing exactly what to say to the rape victim requires skill and sensitivity. For specific examples of helpful conversation, study the chart I've included on the opposite page.

Encourage her trust

Do your best to establish a trusting relationship. Tell her your name, if you haven't done so already, and reassure her that you'll stay with her during the examination. Try to assess her level of understanding; then use words and terms she knows. If you find this difficult, ask yourself: "Am I hiding behind professional jargon and technical terms to cope with my feelings?" Try to find another way to cope. Remember, you add to the patient's distress by making her feel ignorant.

Does your patient seem uncooperative or hostile? Try to be understanding. Consider what may be causing these reactions. For example, ask yourself:
• What happened exactly during the assault?
• How does this patient perceive the rape?
• How is she coping with it? Does she think she's to blame for the attack?
• Are her usual support systems available to her? If not, are they unavailable because of her specific reactions or attitudes toward rape?
• Has this patient received adequate emotional support from you and other health-care professionals?
• Have you and others tried to preserve the patient's dignity and prevent further humiliation?

Supply her needs

Take her to a private area. Then, if you can, find out what your patient really wants. Expectations may vary depending on her perception of the rape. For example, does she primarily seek physical care? Police intervention? Or emotional support? Chances are, she wants all three, but one will take top priority.

To determine this, listen carefully and show your concern. Ask: "How can I help you most?" If she feels threatened by

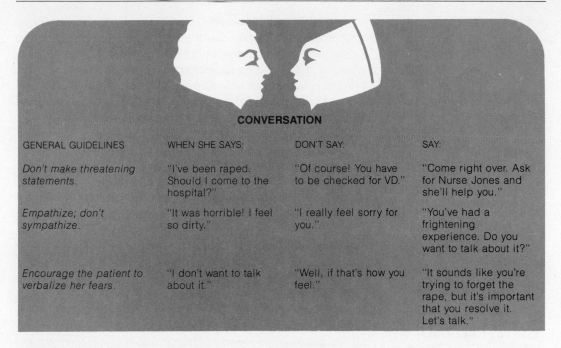

CONVERSATION

GENERAL GUIDELINES	WHEN SHE SAYS:	DON'T SAY:	SAY:
Don't make threatening statements.	"I've been raped. Should I come to the hospital?"	"Of course! You have to be checked for VD."	"Come right over. Ask for Nurse Jones and she'll help you."
Empathize; don't sympathize.	"It was horrible! I feel so dirty."	"I really feel sorry for you."	"You've had a frightening experience. Do you want to talk about it?"
Encourage the patient to verbalize her fears.	"I don't want to talk about it."	"Well, if that's how you feel."	"It sounds like you're trying to forget the rape, but it's important that you resolve it. Let's talk."

others in the emergency department, try to find some privacy. Then encourage her to talk, so you can accurately assess her balancing factors.

Never rush her or give her the impression you're pressuring her. During this critical period, force of any kind will only remind her of the rape.

Nursing tip: Suppose the doctor orders a sedative to help her relax? Administer it as soon as possible, but always wait until her drug and alcohol levels have been checked.

Strengthen support systems

For the first couple of hours, consider yourself as the patient's primary support system. Don't leave her alone. If possible, stay with her from the time she's admitted until she's discharged or transferred to another unit. Answer her questions, collect necessary information, and explain procedures. Serve as a liaison between her, other health professionals, and police officers.

Ask if you can call her husband, lover, parents, or friends. If they've accompanied her to the hospital, let them stay with her, except during the physical exam. However, consider her

When a rape victim phones
Suppose you answer the phone in the doctor's office or emergency department and the caller blurts out, "I've been raped." How can you help?

Begin by advising her to come to the hospital immediately. Give her your name and tell her you can help. Then do your best to find out the following:
• Has she suffered any other physical injury?
• Does she need transportation to the hospital, or someone to accompany her?
• Does she want you to call her regular doctor or gynecologist? If you can, find out if he's on the staff, but don't give her the impression you can't help her if he isn't.

Is she too upset to answer your questions coherently? Ask if there's someone else with her that you can talk to. If she's alone, try again to calm her. Get the address she's calling from, if you can, and tell her you'll send help.

Before you hang up, give her these additional instructions:
• Don't bathe or shower before you come to the hospital.
• Don't change your clothing, or put on make-up. Bring what you need with you.
• Don't take any tranquilizers or drink alcohol.
• Don't empty your bladder or bowels, unless necessary.

When she arrives, be understanding if she's forgotten some of what you told her. Don't add to her stress by scolding her for not following instructions.

individual wishes. Does she prefer privacy during the interview too? Provide it, so you don't intensify her distress.

Pay particular attention to the needs of a child or adolescent who's a rape victim. If her parents are her major support system, ask them to stay throughout the entire examination. Never let anyone tell them to wait outside. To prevent crisis, you must strengthen a patient's balancing factors, not weaken them.

The physical examination
When you've completed your initial assessment, prepare the patient for the physical examination. Before you do, assess her psychologic ability to tolerate a pelvic exam at this time. *The additional stress may trigger repeat flashes of the rape and precipitate a crisis.*

First, find out whether she's ever had such an exam. Remember, she may not have, particularly if she's under age 20. Explain exactly what it includes, why it must be performed, and what's expected of her. Go over each step carefully, repeating your explanation if necessary. Encourage her to ask all the questions she wants before proceeding further. Answer honestly and reassuringly. Urge her to relax, if she can, to make the examination easier.

Keeping the records straight
Ask the patient to sign the necessary consent form. The doctor will need it before he can take her history, perform a pelvic exam, collect rape evidence, and treat her.

Throughout her stay in the emergency department, document all findings carefully. *Important:* Watch what you write on her record, because it may later be used as legal evidence. For example, don't write *alleged* rape. Instead, write *reported* rape. The word *alleged* suggests you have some doubt that she was raped. The word *reported* has no negative connotation.

Collecting evidence: What's your role?
As soon as the doctor arrives, he'll begin taking the patient's history. Some of the questions he'll ask may embarrass her, so stay nearby and offer emotional support. How much information the doctor will need about the rape itself will vary, depending on hospital policy. However, he will need the an-

swers to the following questions, and may ask you to collect and record the facts. Here are some of the questions:

- When was your last menstrual period?
- What method of contraception do you use, if any? If you use oral contraceptives, have you missed any doses?
- What was the time and date of your last voluntary intercourse? Was a condom used?
- Have you ever had gynecologic surgery? What for, and how recently?

Is the history complete? Reassess your patient's stress level before the doctor begins his physical examination. If necessary, explain the procedure again and answer any questions. Tell her what the doctor will look for and why he needs it.

Immediately before the examination, the doctor will probably want a urine sample and blood samples to check for pregnancy and venereal disease, as well as alcohol and drug levels. Important: Always read the hospital's policy in such cases before getting a blood sample. If test results may be used as legal evidence, the procedure may have to be witnessed by a police officer.

Make sure the urine sample isn't a clean catch or midstream specimen. Why? You'll need the entire specimen. And you must not wash away any rape evidence.

Collect the instruments the doctor will need for a pelvic examination. If your hospital uses a rape evidence collection kit, be sure to include it. When you prepare the speculum, don't use lubricant jelly because it will significantly retard sperm motility.

As the doctor examines the patient, stay with her and encourage her to relax. Tell her to breathe slowly through her mouth. Stand near her head so she can see and talk to you. Later, collect further evidence by completing these steps:

- Note condition of patient's clothing. Is it torn? Soiled with semen? Stained with blood? Document your observations carefully. To do this properly, describe the color and size of the stain. Never write what you think caused it.
- Make sure the patient has clean clothing to wear home. Then, collect all torn or soiled clothing. Later, you'll place each piece in an individual *unwaxed paper* bag or container and label it. Remember, this evidence may later be used in court.

Little things mean a lot

To ease a female rape victim's distress, pay attention to the little ways you can make her more comfortable during the doctor's examination. Here are some suggestions:

- Include her in your conversation with the doctor. Continue to call her by name; don't refer to her indirectly as if she's not there. Don't show unconcern by discussing other matters with the doctor.
- Place a pillow under her head.
- Keep her body and legs covered as much as possible. Expose only those areas being examined.
- Make sure the doctor's examining instruments are warmed to room temperature.
- If she's breathing rapidly from nervousness, help her to slow her breathing rate by suggesting that she time her breaths to yours.
- Stay with her for a few minutes after the examination. Help her dress and reassure her. Remember, the examination itself could cause a flashback of her assault.

PREGNANCY AND RAPE
PATIENT TEACHING AID

Dear Patient,

You may become pregnant from the rape. Before deciding what to do about it, find out if you were pregnant *before* the rape. The doctor will help you determine this, possibly with a pregnancy test. Tell him: when your last menstrual period began; how long it lasted; what contraceptive method, if any, you're using.

If you miss a period after the rape, or notice any other signs of pregnancy, like sore breasts or morning sickness, return for a second test.

If you're sure you weren't pregnant at the time you were raped, you may want to take diethylstilbestrol (DES)—the "morning-after pill"—to prevent pregnancy. If you do, take it for as long as your doctor orders. But be sure to read the package insert you'll receive with the drug.

Suppose you do become pregnant from the rape? You can get a legal abortion, if you want, by calling your doctor. However, if you don't want to end the pregnancy, ask him or the hospital's social service agency to discuss some of the other alternatives, such as giving up the baby for adoption.

Important: You may also get a venereal disease (V.D.) from the rape. Because this can be passed on to an unborn baby, ask your doctor or nurse for more information.

VENEREAL DISEASE (V.D.)
PATIENT TEACHING AID

Dear Patient,

You may get a venereal disease (V.D.) from being raped. To guard against it, you've been given an antibiotic. Take it as directed and return to your doctor for further tests.

During the next 4 months, watch for these danger signs and call your doctor if they occur:

• painless sore or discomfort in your vagina, mouth, anus
• skin rash of small round spots or bumps anywhere on the body
• unusual vaginal discharge or odor
• a burning feeling during urination, or swelling at the opening of the urinary tract
• discomfort in the lower back or abdomen, enlarged glands, headaches, appetite loss, nausea, and pain in bones or joints.

Important: You can have V.D. without noticing any of these symptoms. Because you can't be sure until you've had all the tests, avoid infecting others. Be sure to return for further tests.

• Keep her underpants separate from the other garments. Place them in a large enough container so they won't be crumpled.

• Is any clothing wet? Air dry it, if possible. Don't use a fan or electric heater.

• Circle all stains and wet areas on clothing with a laundry marker. Document your observations. Before placing it in a bag or container, put a clean paper over each stain so it won't spread to a clean area. Never fold clothing over a stain.

• Collect any sanitary napkin or tampon present.

• Save any material she may have secured from her attacker: for example, a piece of skin, hair, buttons, or clothing.

• Check to make sure all containers are sealed and labeled. Date and mark each one with your initials. Document it in your notes.

After the exam

When the doctor's finished his physical examination, follow up by helping your patient prepare for discharge. In most cases, you'll probably want to call in a crisis intervention specialist.

Consider her immediate needs. If she's like most women who've been raped, she probably feels dirty and will want to wash. Provide her with any help she needs, as well as lots of warm water, soap, and towels. Offer mouthwash to the patient who's been forced to have oral sex.

Does she want something to eat or drink? Try to get it. Then ask her if she needs extra tissues, money for a phone call, additional clothing.

When she's had time to relax a little, encourage her to ask questions about things that may be bothering her. For example, is she afraid she'll contract a venereal disease from her attacker? Is she worried that she'll become pregnant? Discuss it. Then, to help her explore her options, provide her with an appropriate patient teaching card like the ones illustrated on the opposite page.

Make sure she has a ride home. If she doesn't want you to contact her family or friends, call the hospital's social service department. When a caseworker or aide arrives, give the patient a chance to establish rapport with her. Never insist she get into a car with someone she distrusts. And don't send her home alone in a bus or taxi.

DOMESTIC VIOLENCE: WHAT'S YOUR ROLE?

You're working the day shift in the Emergency Department when 25-year-old Joy Chapman comes in with a swollen, discolored face and severe bruises around her midsection. "I caught my heel in the carpet and fell down the stairs," she says, avoiding eye contact. What do you think of her story? Is she telling the truth?

She may not be. Consider the explanation Ms. Chapman's given for her injuries. Would such a fall cause multiple bruises on her abdomen, the small of her back, and her face? Probably not. Chances are, she was beaten by her husband or boyfriend.

What can you do? First, take her to a private area where you can talk to her. Assess her balancing factors and determine whether she perceives her situation realistically. Like Joy Chapman, a battered woman may try to conceal what really happened because of fear or unwarranted shame. Or, overwhelmed with irrational guilt, she may even believe she "asked for" what she got. Tragically, such a woman's likely to submit to further abuse.

For one reason or another, she may not be able to lean on her usual support systems. Perhaps she's ashamed to confide in friends. And her immediate family may be of no help: Her children are probably frightened and bewildered themselves.

That leaves you. You may be the only real support a battered woman has when she comes to the hospital. Even if she doesn't ask for your help, you'll probably want to offer it. And rightly so—in too many instances, wife beating results in homicide.

Encourage her to speak openly about her fears and frustrations. Your own feelings of anger—both at the husband, and at her for tolerating him—are perfectly natural. But don't let them intrude on your already distraught patient. Avoid making judgmental statements like "Why do you let him hit you?" or "How can you stay with him?" Because she has ambivalent feelings toward her husband, your anger at him may be greater than her own. Such remarks will only put her on the defensive and further threaten her shaky self-image.

If she's given you an implausible explanation for her injuries, tactfully express skepticism: "It's hard for me to see how you could've hurt yourself this way by falling downstairs."

Help her decide what to do. You can't tell her what course of action's best for her, but you can help her explore the options. To do so, try questions like "What else can we do to help you?"

Discuss ways she can alter the destructive pattern of her home life. For example, she can cope by:
• *Taking legal action.* Inform her that the police can issue emergency 24-hour restraining orders to protect her. Even if she doesn't want to press charges, you're probably required to call the police in cases of suspected assault. If so, let her know what you're doing and why. Check your hospital's policies for guidelines.
• *Seeking help from friends and relatives.* A temporary haven with supportive loved ones can lessen your patient's immediate danger and give her time to weigh long-term op-

tions. Ask her who can help, then offer to call them.
• *Going to a shelter.* A temporary residence that's specifically designed to help the battered woman and her children generally provides many services. Besides helping with food, clothing, and housing, it may also offer legal and psychologic counseling, child care, medical assistance, and a 24-hour hotline service. To contact such a shelter, call your hospital's crisis intervention center.

Don't overlook the other services offered by social agencies and your own hospital. If a woman wants to work things out with her husband, she may welcome counseling by a psychologist or social worker.

Even if she resists help, give her a written list of contacts to take with her. She may change her mind later.

If she returns home
Despite your best efforts, your patient may decide to return home, almost certainly to suffer more battering. Try to understand why. Recognizing her reasons may help you deal with your own frustrations at her choice. For example, she may return home because of:
• financial or emotional dependence on her spouse
• concern for her children
• shame over her marriage failure
• fear of retaliation.

Remember, although most battered spouses are women, you may also see male victims, both homosexual and heterosexual. No matter what the patient's sex, the same general guidelines for helping apply.

—BETTY L. LANDON, RN, BA

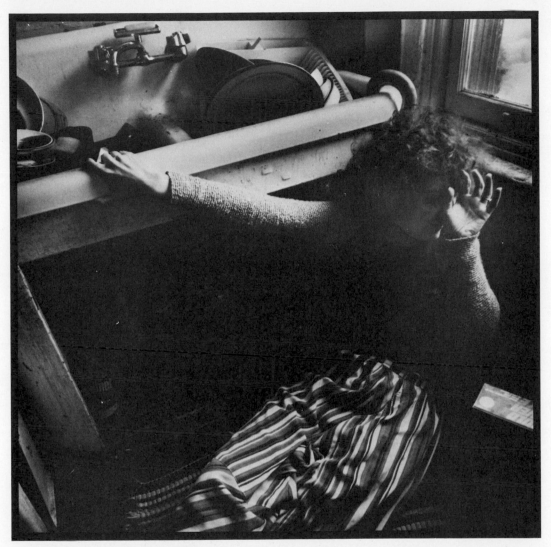

"You may be the only real support a battered woman has when she comes to the hospital. Even if she doesn't ask for your help, offer it."

Another possibility: Ask her to wait till the end of your shift and take her home yourself. She may appreciate this even more, especially if you've established a rapport with her.

Follow up

Before she leaves, urge the patient to see her own doctor for a follow-up exam. If she has no doctor, try to schedule an appointment with one at the hospital. Did the examining doctor order a tranquilizer or sedative? Make sure she has it and teach her everything she should know about the medication.

Show your concern by asking her to call you when she gets home. If possible, arrange for someone to stay with her until she gets over her acute anxiety. Give her the names and local phone numbers of helpful organizations that offer free counseling to rape victims: for example, Women Organized Against Rape (WOAR) or your community's rape crisis center.

As you already know, a little compassion and sensitivity can work wonders when you're caring for a rape victim. But they can't erase the memory of the incident or eliminate all stress and fear. No matter how busy you are, never forget the patient has had a dehumanizing, emotionally shattering experience. Try to imagine how you'd feel after an assault. Then do your best to give her the tender sensitive care she deserves.

Where to refer the patient and her family

Check your phone book for the names and phone numbers of counseling services for the rape victim, as well as shelters for victims of domestic violence. Two such local organizations are Women Organized Against Rape (WOAR), 1220 Sansom Street, Philadelphia, Pa. 19107. Phone: 215-922-3434, and Women Against Abuse, P.O. Box 12233, Philadelphia, Pa. 19144. Phone: 215-386-7777. You may also write to the following organizations for information:

• Center for Women Policy Studies, 200 P Street NW, Suite 508, Washington, D.C. 20036

• Rape Crisis Center, Box 21005, Washington, D.C. 20009. Phone: 202-333-7273

9

Managing the alcoholic and drug abuser

BY LANIGHTA LEWIS, RN

FEW PATIENTS ARE MORE vulnerable to crises than alcoholics and drug abusers. And few patients offer greater challenges than these—challenges to your nursing skills, to your capacity to understand other people, and to your ability to cope with your own feelings. With more and more such patients being admitted to hospitals, you're going to face these challenges. Can you meet them?

Read this chapter. It'll help you:

• Explore and accept your feelings about alcohol and drug abuse.

• Recognize alcoholics and drug abusers.

• Identify their needs.

• Plan interventions to help them maintain their equilibrium while in your care.

Imagine yourself caring for 38-year-old Mrs. Fields, who's just had a ureteral lithotomy. After her operation, she has an uneventful recovery for the first 48 hours, except for transient confusion and irritability. Then, unexpectedly, she goes into DTs, and you hurt your wrist trying to restrain her.

Afterwards, you realize that your feelings of hurt and anger go back beyond the incident itself. You start to reexamine

Keys to identification

If you observe someone with these signs, suspect alcoholism:
- alcoholic breath odor
- facial edema
- slurred speech
- poor coordination
- a broad-based, footdrop/slapping walk
- visual disturbances, such as blurred vision; bloodshot eyes
- GI distress: nausea, vomiting, anorexia, diarrhea
- insomnia.

On the first day of alcohol withdrawal, expect him to have:
- coarse tremor of hands, face, sometimes his entire body
- increased blood pressure; tachycardia
- low-grade fever
- diaphoresis or dehydration
- nervousness and agitation.

Important: Watch for signs of depression. If it's severe enough, the patient may attempt suicide.

your attitude toward alcoholics. Are alcoholics more difficult to care for than other patients? If so, why?

A problem of perception

If you'd known that Mrs. Fields was an alcoholic, you might have prevented the crisis that led to her combative behavior. But you didn't know until she went into DTs. Why didn't you? Was it a problem of perception? If you're not sure, consider some reasons why your perception of the alcoholic may be inaccurate.

- *Faulty assessment.* You probably know already that there's no such thing as the "typical alcoholic." Even the patient who's obviously intoxicated when he's admitted to the hospital isn't necessarily an alcoholic. The alcoholic usually looks just like any other patient. Furthermore, he's commonly admitted under a secondary or false diagnosis such as gastritis. So you may not recognize what his real problem is—unless you know alcoholism's special signs and symptoms. Later on, I'll explain exactly what these are.

- *A sense of failure.* When a patient's condition doesn't improve despite your best efforts, you may feel like you've failed. In a general hospital, you may not see any long-term success with alcoholics. Instead, you may see a high readmission rate. Unless your expectations are realistic, you may try to protect yourself from feelings of frustration and insecurity by categorizing all alcoholics as "hopeless."

- *Lack of objectivity.* Alcoholism is so widespread that you, like many other nurses, may have trouble seeing alcoholic patients objectively. Perhaps a family member, or a close friend, drinks excessively. If so, you must try to detach yourself from your own feelings about it enough to view your alcoholic patients fairly. Remember, many alcoholics do have the courage and willpower to recover and lead productive lives. Do your best to view the alcoholic as a person with a problem, not as a weak character or an affront to morality.

Coping with the truth

Yes, psychologic stumbling blocks can impair your ability to spot the alcoholic patient and help him deal with his problems effectively. Denial is one such stumbling block. You'll recognize this in yourself when:

- You don't see the patient as a whole person but as a col-

"It's not always easy to identify the alcoholic patient. But if you don't intervene before he goes into withdrawal, he may become defensive, hostile, and even combative."

Watch for complications
During withdrawal, a patient who's seriously debilitated may have any of these potentially lethal complications:
● coronary problems
● upper respiratory problems
● liver failure
● severe electrolyte imbalance
● convulsions.
    Observe your patient closely and inform the doctor immediately of any change in his condition.

lection of signs and symptoms. By attributing each of these to various causes, you "explain away" the patient, symptom by symptom.

● You manage each of alcoholism's signs as a separate problem. Following doctor's orders, you medicate him for restlessness; restrain him for confusion; feed and nurture him for malnutrition. In this way, you neglect the common underlying factor.

● You ignore the patient's emotional needs and care only for physical complaints.

The trouble with denial and other psychologic defenses is they interfere with your perception. When this happens, you leave your alcoholic patient without the support that could help restore his equilibrium.

Deprived of familiar surroundings and his usual coping mechanisms, he's probably acutely sensitive to the people around him. He'll quickly see through any facade you might use to hide your aversion to him. In defense, he may become hostile, exaggerate his complaints, or become increasingly dependent. If you then ask the doctor to order narcotics and restraints to control his behavior, you've just confirmed that the alcoholic's a difficult patient.

Now let's discuss how you can change this picture. To do this, you have to strengthen your own balancing factors. Learn to recognize the alcoholic patient and the drug abuser. For easy reference, I've isolated all the information about drug abuse on page 136. And in the margin on page 132 are ways to try to identify the alcoholic patient during your initial interview.

Recognizing the alcoholic patient
As I've already mentioned, even the patient who's obviously intoxicated when admitted isn't necessarily an alcoholic. However, be suspicious. And always document your observation. Then, if he develops withdrawal signs and symptoms 18 hours later he won't take everyone by surprise. Besides recording the patient's condition, tell his doctor what you've seen. His reaction will determine your next step. For example, the doctor may order a sedative to minimize withdrawal signs. Later, I'll explain just what form these withdrawal signs usually take and how to deal with them.

The patient's behavior may also furnish clues about his

drinking habits. For example:

• *He may fail to respond to standard doses of medication.* The patient who's apparently unaffected by normal doses of analgesics, tranquilizers, or surgical anesthetics may have a cross-tolerance to these medications because of alcoholism. On the other hand, he may be profoundly affected by even a small dose. Ask him about his drinking habits. You may discover he's an alcoholic.

• *He may have predictable mood swings.* After a night of abstinence, an alcoholic may develop withdrawal symptoms: tremors, nausea, vomiting, and hypersensitivity to stimuli. Because he can't get his own alcohol to relieve his discomfort, the alcoholic may depend on family or friends for it. Such patients may grow agitated and tremulous before visiting hours, then become calm, even euphoric afterwards. I remember one case where the half-gallons of freshly squeezed orange juice a family brought daily were liberally laced with vodka. So was the coffee brought in by another family.

Keep an eye on patients with a lot of mouthwash or toiletries. One patient I remember developed DTs after 2 weeks in the hospital. The source of his alcohol? Seven bottles of mouthwash he'd hidden and consumed.

After recognition comes reaction

If you can recognize the alcoholic patient, you've got an important balancing factor working for you. But to truly effectively cope with him, you must cope first with your own reactions.

Imagine yourself caring for Dan Patton, a 50-year-old business executive who's just returned to your unit after surgery. The doctor's ordered you to withhold sedation until Mr. Patton becomes alert. As you check his condition, you observe that his recovery from anesthesia's unusually prolonged. Several hours later, his blood pressure, temperature, and respirations rise and he becomes confused. Suddenly, he begins having visual hallucinations and acting out combatively. When your attempts to reorient him fail, you call his doctor for restraining orders. "Go ahead," he says. "You'll need more than restraints before the night's over. He's a drinker. How about if I order some Librium?"

What's your first reaction? Perhaps you thought you had the situation under control; now you find out Mr. Patton's

DEALING WITH THE DRUG ABUSE PATIENT

The next drug addicted patient you see may be a business executive, a housewife, a senior citizen, or a grade school student. Surprised? Don't be. Drug addiction occurs in all types of people of all ages.

People take drugs for many reasons. Some want to escape problems or situations they can't cope with. Others seek pleasure and want to stimulate their senses. Some use drugs to defy their parents or other authority figures. Others take them to relieve physical symptoms, real or imagined. Still others become addicted inadvertently when they take drugs for long-term illness.

Identifying the abuser

How can you tell if your patient is addicted to narcotics? Watch for:
• runny nose
• unsteady walk
• wan, undernourished appearance
• bloodshot eyes; dilated or constricted pupils
• involuntary rapid eye movement
• slurred speech

• emotional outbursts
• profuse or unnatural sweating
• track marks on inside of arms or, less commonly, under tongue or toenails
• long-sleeved clothing in hot weather.

Suspect addiction if you discover the patient knows a lot about specific drugs and their effects. Maybe he'll tell you he's allergic to the milder pain-killing drugs like Darvon, Demerol, or Codeine. Remember, specialized knowledge or high drug tolerances may come from experimentation and unprescribed use.

Sometimes a patient complains of pain but can't tell you where it hurts. Others may make up symptoms to get drugs, like the man who complained of kidney stone discomfort but showed no trace of blood in his urine.

Caring for the abuser

If you suspect your patient's addicted to drugs, notify the patient's doctor. If the patient's scheduled for surgery, call his anesthesiologist too. The doctor will decide whether or not to

treat the patient for addiction. If he does, the treatment will vary with the specific drug and the severity of addiction. But whatever the course of treatment, you can help your patient by following these general guidelines:
• Don't let the patient or his family manipulate you. He may refuse to do what you ask unless you give him what he wants. Don't ignore his demands, but don't give in either. Similarly, the family may try to dictate how you handle his care. Listen, but don't surrender control.
• Don't pass judgment or impose your morals on the patient. If you feel hostile or contemptuous towards him, he'll sense it. Once he becomes defensive or withdrawn, chances for developing a rapport are remote.
• Remember, normal dosages of medication may not affect the addicted patient. Keep the doctor informed about the patient's reaction to drugs. He may tell you to increase or decrease the dosage and frequency of the medication, depending on the treatment plan.

Neonatal narcotic withdrawal

The fetus of a woman addicted to narcotics is also likely to be addicted. As you know, many drugs cross the placental barrier, increasing the chance of premature birth and retarding growth.

About half of all infants born to addicted women are smaller than average, including those that are premature. The addicted infant, in addition, shows these typical withdrawal signs: cyanosis, trembling, convulsions, muscular rigidity, and gastrointestinal disorders. His cries are shrill and high-pitched.

How can you help the addicted infant?

• Give him prescribed sedation to help him sleep. Treatment usually lasts for two five-day periods, with full dosage the first period, then a gradual reduction in dosage until the withdrawal symptoms disappear. For severe cases, the doctor may prescribe paregoric; for milder cases, phenobarbital or chlorpromazine.
• Care for him gently; don't jostle the crib or make sudden movements. Don't avoid physical contact with the child. He needs to be held and loved like any newborn.

• Put soft mittens on his hands to keep him from scratching himself.

Fetal alcohol syndrome

According to recent studies, an alcoholic's chance of spontaneous abortion or giving birth to a deformed infant is significant. One-third of the newborns of alcoholics are shorter than normal, with heads proportionally even smaller. Usually, the affected infant is mentally deficient. One out of ten infants has disharmonic eye and midfacial development and about 4% have a ventricular septal defect.

"Drug abuse has become a relatively common phenomenon. Don't be surprised to find it in people of all ages."

	CONTROLLED SUBSTANCES: USES AND EFFECTS					
	DRUGS BRAND NAME	USE	DEPENDENCE POTENTIAL: (physical and psycho-logical)	USUAL METHODS OF ADMINIS-TRATION	POSSIBLE EFFECTS	SIGNS OF WITHDRAWAL
NARCOTICS	**opium** Dover's Powder, Paregoric	Analgesic, antidiarrheal	High	Oral, smoked	Euphoria, drowsi-ness, respiratory depression, Cheyne-Stokes respiration, nausea, pupillary changes. *Overdose:* Slow and shallow breathing, clammy skin, convul-sions, coma, possi-ble death.	Watery eyes, runny nose, yawning, loss of appetite, irrita-bility, tremors, panic, chills and sweating, cramps, nausea, vomiting, diarrhea, dilated pupils, nightmares, tachycardia.
	morphine Morphine	Analgesic	High	Injected, smoked		
	codeine Codeine	Analgesic, an-titussive	Moderate	Oral, injected		
	heroin	None	High	Injected, sniffed		
	meperidine (Pethidine) Demerol, Pethadol	Analgesic	High	Oral, injected		
	methadone Dolophine, Methadone, Methadose	Analgesic, heroin substi-tute	High	Oral, injected		
	Other Dilaudid, Leritine, Numorphan, Percodan	Analgesic, antidiarrheal, antitussive	High	Oral, injected		
DEPRESSANTS	**chloral hydrate** Noctec, Som-nos	Hypnotic	Moderate	Oral	Slurred speech, disorientation, drunken behavior without odor of alco-hol, ataxia, nystag-mus. *Overdose:* Shallow respiration, cold and clammy skin, weak and rapid pulse, de-creased deep ten-don reflexes, coma, death.	Anxiety, insomnia, tremors, delirium, convulsions, weak-ness, fever, possi-ble death.
	barbiturates Amytal, Butisol, Nembutal, Pheno-barbital, Seconal, Tuinal	Anesthetic, anti-convulsant, sedation, sleep	High	Oral, injected		
	glutethimide Doriden	Sedation, sleep	High	Oral		

CONTROLLED SUBSTANCES: USES AND EFFECTS					
DRUGS BRAND NAME	USE	DEPENDENCE POTENTIAL: (physical and psycho-logical)	USUAL METHODS OF ADMINIS-TRATION	POSSIBLE EFFECTS	SIGNS OF WITHDRAWAL
DEPRESSANTS					
methaqualone Optimil, Parest, Quaalude, Somnafac, Sopor	Sedation, sleep	High	Oral	*Methaqualone overdose*: hyperirritability, increased deep tendon reflexes, dilated pupils.	
tranquilizers Equanil, Librium, Miltown, Serax, Tranxene, Valium	Antianxiety, muscle relaxant, sedation	High	Oral		
STIMULANTS					
cocaine Cocaine	Local anesthetic	Possible/high	Injected, sniffed	Increased alertness, excitation, euphoria, paranoia, dilated pupils, increased pulse rate and blood pressure, insomnia, loss of appetite. *Overdose*: Agitation, tremor, increased body temperature, shallow respirations, arrhythmias, halluci-nations, convulsions, possible death.	Apathy, long peri-ods of sleep, irrita-bility, depression, disorientation. With long-standing addiction, patient will experience abdominal and muscular cramps, nausea, vomiting, and severe agita-tion.
amphetamines Benzedrine, Biphetamine, Desoxyn, Dex-edrine	Hyperkinesis, narcolepsy, weight control	Possible/high	Oral, injected		
phenmetrazine Preludin	Weight control	Possible/high	Oral		
methylpheni-date Ritalin	Hyperkinesis	Possible/high	Oral		
Other Cylert, Didrex, Pondimin, Sanorex,	Weight control	Possible	Oral		
CANNABIS					
marijuana hashish, hashish oil	None approved	Degree un-known/ moderate	Oral, smoked	Euphoria, relaxed in-hibitions, increased appetite, disoriented behavior, normal pupils, hypotension, tachycardia. *Overdose*: Fatigue, paranoia, possible psychosis.	Insomnia, hyperac-tivity, and decreased appetite reported in a limited number of individuals.

CONTROLLED SUBSTANCES: USES AND EFFECTS

DRUGS BRAND NAME	USE	DEPENDENCE POTENTIAL: (physical and psychological)	USUAL METHODS OF ADMINIS-TRATION	POSSIBLE EFFECTS	SIGNS OF WITHDRAWAL
LSD	None	None/degree unknown	Oral	Illusions and halluci-nations (with excep-tion of MDA); poor perception of time and distance. *Overdose:* Longer, more intense "trip" episodes, dilated pupils, hypertension, tachycardia, increased deep tendon reflexes, psychosis, possible death.	Withdrawal syn-drome not re-ported.
mescaline	None	None/degree unknown	Oral, injected		
Psilocybin	None	None/degree unknown	Oral		
MDA	None	None/degree unknown	Oral, injected		
PCP Sernylan	Veterinary an-esthetic	None/degree unknown	Oral, injected, smoked, sniffed		

(HALLUCINOGENS)

SLANG TERMS FOR DRUGS: A GLOSSARY

Amphetamines	bennies, copilots, crystal, jelly beans, meth, pep, speed, uppers, wake-ups
Barbiturates	barbs, blues, downers, Mexican reds, nebbies, nimbies, rainbows, red and blues, yellow jackets
Cocaine	big C, coke, gold dust, snow, paradise, dream
Hashish	black Russian, hash, kif, soles
Heroin	big H, duji, horse, powder, smack, scag, stuff
LSD	acid, California sunshine, microdots, strawberry, window pane
Marijuana	acapulco, broccoli, dope, gage, ganja, grass, joint, pot, weed
Mescaline	buttons, cactus mesc, mescal buttons, moon
Methamphetamines	crystal, meth, speed
Methaqualone	quads, ludes, soapers, sopes
Morphine	Miss Emma, first line, mud, morf, morphy
Phencyclidine	angel dust, PCP, peace pill, killer weed (when combined with marijuana)

condition's going to get worse. Whatever your initial reaction, acknowledge it. If you're angry or frustrated, admit it to yourself or share your feelings with another nurse. Then, think of a way to channel those feelings to help the patient. Does the thought of caring for an alcoholic scare you? If so, try to determine why: Is it the physical challenge? Do you feel you don't understand the disease? Be honest with yourself. Then take steps to strengthen your own balancing factors.

Mutual support

Don't overlook another important balancing factor—the mutual support you and other nurses can share. For example:

• Try working together when caring for the alcoholic, instead of by yourself. Double-assigning gives you relief to take a break when you need it, without neglecting your patient.

• Always keep an up-to-date care plan for every alcoholic patient. Include any special tips that may help other nurses care for him.

• Never undo what another nurse has done for the patient. For example, if she's trying to reduce his demand for sedatives by using other nursing measures instead, stick to her plan. If you don't, you're asking for the patient to assume control with manipulative behavior.

Dealing with the patient's denial: A direct approach

We've already touched on how psychologic stumbling-blocks can get in the way. Now let's talk about how the patient's own defense mechanisms can impede his progress toward recovery.

You already know that alcoholism's more than a disease: It's a complex social problem that affects not only the victims, but also their families and the entire community. Paradoxically, our society condones alcohol as a way to ease social encounters and to relieve stress. Yet society tends to condemn people who become dependent on alcohol as an escape mechanism. To be labeled alcoholic is to carry a stigma. Fearful of social disapproval, many alcoholics strive to keep their condition secret and will deny using alcohol excessively if confronted. They may even deceive themselves about how much they consume, and show anger and resentment towards you for asking them.

Yet, asking a patient about his drinking habits is the most direct way to detect alcoholism. To do this, try saying some-

Alcohol withdrawal or drug overdose?

Don't be confused by the resemblance between the toxic withdrawal reaction and the drug overdose reaction. In both types, the patient sleeps constantly and snores, although he can be roused. When awakened, he shows slowed motor response, drowsiness, and confusion.

How can you tell the difference? Check for nystagmus: You'll see it with drug overdose, but not alcohol withdrawal. This is a more reliable clue than whether the patient's vital signs are elevated or depressed. The old rule of thumb about "vital signs elevated in alcohol withdrawal, but depressed in drug overdose" doesn't always hold true. For example, in aspirin overdose, vital signs are elevated.

Remember, for the patient withdrawing from alcohol, this is a dangerous period: He can quickly develop DTs unless he gets adequate tranquilizing medication.

A need for better communication

Naturally, your ability to assess and manage the alcoholic patient will greatly improve with good communication between you and the attending doctor. A doctor should supply you with a history indicating how much alcohol his patient normally consumes, if he knows. With this, you're prepared for possible adverse drug reactions, potentiation, and withdrawal reactions.

Your care plan or Kardex notes should also describe the patient's patterns of alcohol consumption. For instance, "Patient states he drinks one pint of whiskey per day." Only then will the entire health care team be able to anticipate complications, and not be caught unprepared.

thing like this: "How much alcohol you drink is very important. It can influence the choice and amount of medication we give you. Depending on how much alcohol you usually consume, some medications may be ineffective, and others may even make you sick." Then, ask him to estimate his average weekly or daily intake. Document his response in your nursing notes. If the amount he drinks seems excessive to you, notify the doctor.

Of course, a patient may become angry when you discover he has a drinking problem. For example, during an initial interview I asked Mrs. White to estimate her alcohol intake. She got a panicky look, then anger took over, and she ordered me from her room. Before leaving, I assured her that no one would reproach her for her drinking habits... but that we needed such information to care for her properly. That afternoon she complained to her doctor about her nursing care.

What do you do when such a thing happens? First, have another nurse accompany you whenever you go into the patient's room. Don't let this seem threatening or offensive; just act like it's routine. Having another nurse with you can bolster your self-confidence if the patient becomes abusive or manipulative.

Second, explain the situation to the patient's doctor and the hospital administration; document this on your nurse's notes. Tell them that the patient or family may complain about nursing care. Such information helps the administration to handle any complaints in an informed way, and opens communication in case more information's needed.

Is honesty with the patient worth the risks? Yes. I'm convinced that mentioning your suspicions to the patient does him a favor. Remaining a hidden alcoholic is exhausting and frightening. Time and time again, I've watched an alcoholic patient relax when he realized that someone knew his dreadful secret. In other cases, a patient's initial denial and anger give way to honest discussions later. A direct approach may prompt your patients to seek the long-term treatment they need. In any case, your know-how permits you to plan and give better care. It can even save a life.

Consider Mrs. Fields, the patient I mentioned at the beginning of this chapter. Mrs. Fields was an alcoholic. Without an adequate blood level of alcohol and without proper medical management, she had gone into withdrawal and DTs, a potentially lethal complication. If her condition had been recognized and reported, the doctor would have delayed surgery until she'd completed alcohol withdrawal. In case of emergency surgery, a different anesthetic agent and special postop care would have reduced the chances of DTs.

Helping the patient through acute withdrawal

Now that we've considered how to recognize the alcoholic patient and deal with some of your psychologic stumbling-blocks, let's consider specific ways to help an alcoholic patient go through withdrawal.

Depending on how long he's been drinking and how much he's consumed, expect to see withdrawal signs developing within 12 to 48 hours after he stops drinking. Unless you recognize these signs promptly and take the right steps, he may develop DTs. What can you do to prevent it? Recognize that the patient will need medication as well as your emotional support. During the acute stage of withdrawal which can last as long as 5 days, he'll be anxious and irritable. To relieve his discomfort, the doctor will probably order a tranquilizer such as chlordiazepoxide (Librium) or diazepam (Valium). Whatever the medication, give it as often as ordered unless the patient shows toxic effects.

Expect uncooperative, disruptive behavior. When it occurs, don't waste time trying to talk the patient out of it, because you may not succeed. Instead, tell him that you're going to give him tranquilizing medication and try to establish a relaxed atmosphere. Speak slowly and calmly. Watch his reactions. To protect him from injury don't leave before his medication takes effect. Doing so may increase his anxiety and trigger confusion.

Coping with physical problems

Now, let's discuss how to care for physical problems during withdrawal.

As the patient's blood alcohol level starts to fall, he'll probably become overhydrated; this is because his body's become dependent on alcohol's diuretic effect to maintain fluid balance. Usually, this condition reverses itself in a day or two and requires no intervention.

However, the vomiting and diarrhea common during alcohol withdrawal can cause serious electrolyte imbalances, partic-

Dealing with manipulative behavior
Expect manipulative behavior and recognize it as a plea for consistency, a search for someone the patient can trust. Know what forms it may take, and what to do about it:
• Frequent physical complaints: Giving medication for psychosomatic discomfort merely continues what the patient's been doing for himself with alcohol: denying his real problem. Instead, reassure him that his discomfort will decrease as withdrawal is complete. When he understands the reason for his physical discomfort, he'll probably be less anxious, although he will be uncomfortable for the next few days.
• Attempts to provoke hospital staff: Taking provocative remarks personally allows the patient to control you. Don't be trapped into reacting, particularly to complaints about other nurses.

CARING FOR THE PATIENT WITH DTs

Watch closely for signs of DTs, the most serious danger to withdrawal patients. Even with expert care, about 15% of afflicted patients will die, usually from hyperthermia or circulatory collapse.

DTs are characterized by severe psychomotor agitation, confusion, and disorientation, and frightening and threatening hallucinations. Vital signs are elevated. Signs of autonomic nervous system disorders develop, such as dilated pupils, fever, tachycardia, and profuse sweating. Generalized seizures, usually grand mal, may begin; some doctors prescribe anticonvulsants as a preventive measure. Other doctors may use them to ameliorate the seizures once they've started. *Nursing tip:* Tape a padded tongue depressor to the head of the bed for easy availability in case of seizure.

The best treatment is prevention by medicating and soothing the patient during alcohol withdrawal. Follow these guidelines:
• Provide a calm, nonstressful atmosphere.
• Reassure the patient that his hallucinations are only imaginary, and will stop once he's completed withdrawal.
• Maintain his fluid and electrolyte balance.
• Control nausea and vomiting to prevent complications such as massive GI bleeding or rupture of the esophagus.
• Give *adequate* sedation to relieve CNS irritability. *Note:* Alcoholics may mimic agitated psychotics in that they may need several times the normal amount of sedation during the most acute phase of withdrawal. Have emergency resuscitation devices available in case of overmedication.

Remember, the patient in DTs is out of touch with reality.

He is dangerous to himself and everyone else. Arrange for transfer to a protective environment. Meanwhile, confine the patient to an area where he's least likely to harm himself or others should he become combative. Use restraints, if necessary; get the doctor's permission and document that you've done so. For more information on the combative patient, see pages 82 to 85.

Nursing tips on hallucinosis
When caring for the patient in hallucinosis, follow these suggestions:
• Keep the room well lit; close closet and bathroom doors to avoid shadows.
• Shut out loud noises. Keep people from coming in the room unnecessarily. Discourage intercom use in the patient's room.
• Refer frequently to the patient's actual surroundings in conversation.

ANTABUSE
PATIENT TEACHING AID

Dear Patient:
The doctor has prescribed Antabuse (disulfiram) to help you eliminate your intake of alcohol. Most patients tolerate the drug well, but you may suffer side effects such as drowsiness, fatigue, impotence, skin eruptions, and metallic aftertaste. These will disappear as your body adjusts to the drug.

Antabuse interferes with the breakdown of alcohol. Should you take a drink, toxic levels of acetaldehyde accumulate and produce a rapid, intense, and unpleasant reaction. Caution: The reaction may even be fatal. Even a small amount of alcohol can produce the reaction, so be sure not to take alcohol-containing drugs such as Paregoric, Nyquil, Nervine, or liquid vitamins. Dilantin and paraldehyde may also cause a reaction. The patient who's having a reaction usually has:
• severe nausea and vomiting
• hypotension
• rapid pulse and respirations
• flushed face
• bloodshot eyes.
The Antabuse reaction may last as long as there's alcohol in the blood. Because of the severity of the alcohol-Antabuse reaction, Antabuse is not recommended for patients with serious heart disease, serious mental illness, diabetes, epilepsy, or serious liver impairment.

"DTs pose a serious danger to withdrawal patients. The condition's characterized by severe psychomotor agitation, confusion, and frightening hallucinations."

ularly hypokalemia. To combat severe GI distress, the doctor may order an antiemetic such as promethazine (Phenergan) and an antidiarrheal such as Kaopectate.

Besides giving medications, see that your patient has a well-balanced diet.

Proper nutrition, including multiple-vitamin supplements, will help correct metabolic imbalances and any existing dietary deficiencies. If the patient can't tolerate full meals, offer him snacks appropriate to his diet at least every 4 to 6 hours.

After the first 2 days, the patient may have such profuse sweating and diuresis that he becomes dehydrated. To prevent this, give fruit-flavored drinks reinforced with amino acids and sugar: for example, Gatorade. Such a mixture is easily digested, maintains electrolyte balance, and maintains a high blood-sugar level. When blood sugar levels drop as they do during withdrawal, the patient's tremors will become more severe. Offer 8 ounces of fluid every 2 hours during the withdrawal period, and keep careful intake and output records. Avoid I.V. fluids if possible, so that he can stay mobile.

Putting it all together
This chapter has tried to show you how to cope effectively with the alcoholic patient and help him overcome the stress of withdrawal. Remember, the way to avoid potential crises is to anticipate them. Review what I've told you, then deepen your knowledge by exploring the recent literature devoted to this subject. Remember that the enlightened, professional care you give your patient increases his chance for recovery.

Where to refer the patient and his family
For the alcoholic, hospitalization is only the first step. To achieve any lasting benefits, he must undertake a long-term therapy or counseling program for his drinking problem.

Many such programs are now available, including such self-help groups as Alcoholics Anonymous (AA), Alateen, and Al-Anon.

To find other help in your area, contact the local affiliate of the Provincial or National Council on Alcoholism, or your local health department.

SKILLCHECK 2

I. You're a nurse in a maternity delivery room, and you're caring for 28-year-old Tillie Breck, who's just given birth to a 5-pound-boy. When he begins suffering severe respiratory distress, he's quickly transferred to the neonatal ICU. Although Mrs. Breck is still groggy from the anesthetic, she seems aware of the commotion around her. She asks you: "Is something wrong with my baby?" How do you answer?

a) You say, "You'll have to ask your pediatrician." Then you continue to care for her physically until she's transferred to the recovery room.

b) You say, "Your baby has been taken to the ICU, where he'll be cared for by the nurses there."

c) You say, "Right now, your baby is having trouble breathing. The doctor will explain what's being done to help him."

d) You say, "Don't worry about your baby. After you're settled in your room, I'll find out what's happening and tell you."

2. You're caring for 62-year-old Saul Tarsky, who has been fighting a losing battle with cancer of the larynx. He's feeling very weak and has trouble retaining even the small tube feedings you give him. One morning when you're feeding him, he takes his note pad and writes: "That's enough. I don't want you to do anything more for me." When you ask him what he means, he writes: "I'm too tired to struggle anymore. I don't even have the strength to die." What do you do?

a) Stop feeding him at once and leave him alone, so he can rest.

b) Stop feeding him, but sit quietly with him for awhile. Wait until he writes something more on his note pad.

c) Stop feeding him immediately and phone his wife. She'll be able to comfort him.

d) Ask the doctor to change his feeding schedule, so he gets smaller feedings more often.

3. Two days ago, 80-year-old Sara Saunders had surgery to repair a broken hip. She's confined to bed with a Foley catheter. Shortly after you come on duty one night at 11 p.m., she insists on getting out of bed to urinate. When you try to explain why she can't,

she strikes out at you and yells loudly. What's your assessment, and how should you intervene?

a) She's confused because of the pain. You find the resident on duty and have her sedated.

b) She thinks you're someone she dislikes. You leave the room and ask another nurse to take over.

c) She's psychotic and probably can't be reoriented. You restrain her and put the side rails up.

d) She's confused and in crisis. You turn on the lights and try to reorient her.

4. Mr. Reyes, a 55-year-old newspaperman, has disrupted the floor with his demanding behavior. Besides complaining about the care he receives, he uses obscene language and tries to pick fights with you and the other nurses. You:

a) Argue with him when he challenges you. Mr. Reyes is obviously a man who likes to argue. Maybe a frank discussion will clear the air.

b) Touch him as much as possible to reassure him of your support.

c) Listen to his complaints. Keep your own responses brief and calm.

d) Spend as little time as possible with him so he'll know you disapprove of his behavior.

e) b and c above.

5. Mrs. Patrick Moriarity wanted to be fully conscious for the delivery of her first child. But when she had unexpected difficulty during labor, her doctor gave her Demerol for the pain. Now, two days after the birth of a healthy girl, she suddenly seems depressed. When you bring the baby to her for breastfeeding, she starts to cry. "I feel like I've failed as a mother," she wails. Surprised, you try to comfort her. What do you say?

a) You say, "Don't be upset, Mrs. Moriarity. Lots of women get depressed right after childbirth. You'll be okay soon."

b) You ask, "Are you worried about caring for your baby after you take him home?"

c) You say, "Why do you feel you've failed, Mrs. Moriarity?"

d) You talk to her, including all of the above statements.

e) You ask, "Have you spoken to your husband?"

(Answers on page 179)

6. You're a nurse in a clinic. About five months ago, Mrs. John Coburn's baby died suddenly, an apparent victim of sudden infant death syndrome (SIDS). When she comes into the doctor's office for a routine gynecologic checkup, she hesitantly asks you, "Do you think my baby died because he slept in the bureau drawer?" What do you do to help her?

a) Reassure her that the baby didn't die because of where he slept.

b) Give her the address and phone number of the local SIDS chapter.

c) Tell her that parents of SIDS victims usually feel guilty, even though they're not to blame.

d) Explain that victims of SIDS don't die from suffocation, aspiration, regurgitation, or neglect.

e) Ask her how she and her husband feel about the tragedy after five months.

f) All of the above.

7. Roxanne White, a 35-year-old vocalist, is your most demanding patient. She's just had an elective blepharoplasty and must lie very still for the first 16 hours after surgery. Not only must you provide for all her physical needs, but you must also listen to her constant complaining. You and the other nurses are beginning to resent spending so much time with a patient who has come to the hospital for a face lift. What can you do?

a) Tell a member of Ms. White's family about her needs. Ask him to do as much as he can to help her.

b) Put everything Ms. White may need within her reach. Tell her what you've done and ask her to do as much as possible for herself. Explain that you have other patients to care for. Inform her that she may have to wait a few minutes if she needs you to assist her.

c) Recognize that Ms. White's appearance is extremely important to her, or she wouldn't have had cosmetic surgery. Try to understand her needs. Give her as much emotional support and care, as possible. Urge the other nurses to understand Ms. White's needs, too.

d) All of the above, in this order: b, a, c.

e) All of the above, in this order: c, b, a.

8. Maxwell Royer, a 72-year-old retired meat cutter, approaches you one day on the surgical floor and asks how to get up to the hospital's roof. When you inquire why, he urges you to lower your voice and glances about nervously. "I've been receiving messages through my television set," he tells you. "I have an appointment to meet the commander of the Galaxy Patrol in 15 minutes."
What do you do?

a) Tell Mr. Royer that the Galaxy Patrol does not exist. Explain it must be something he imagined.

b) Ask him to tell you more about the Galaxy Patrol. Inquire what it is exactly, and how it functions.

c) Tell Mr. Royer that he's in the hospital and lead him back to his bed.

d) Tell Mr. Royer that he's in the hospital and you're a nurse. Ask him if he remembers coming to the hospital.

9. Ninety-year-old Mrs. Rolando Diaz suffers from severe senile dementia and is constantly confused. All your efforts to reorient her are unsuccessful. One day as you feed her, she becomes convinced that her son, Wayne, is suspended from the ceiling. Convinced he's about to fall, she becomes increasingly frightened and agitated. What's your next step?

a) Tell Mrs. Diaz her son is not on the ceiling. Inform her that if she doesn't eat, she won't get better.

b) Tell her that her son won't fall if she stays calm. Then attempt to quiet her so you can continue feeding her.

c) Ask her to explain exactly what she sees.

d) Tell her she's in the hospital and her son, Wayne, is at home.

10. Eighteen-year-old Richard Goldman is admitted to the hospital after slashing his wrists in a suicide attempt. When you first see him in your unit, you notice that he's awake and alert, but withdrawn. What do you do?

a) Encourage him to talk by asking, "Why did you want to kill yourself?"

b) Conclude that he's probably learned his lesson, since the attempt didn't get him the attention he wanted. Show him you've dismissed the episode by avoiding any discussion about it.

c) Consider him a high-risk suicidal patient and protect him accordingly.

d) Care for him as you would any patient with lacerations. Leave any psychologic counselling he needs to his doctor and social worker.

(Answers on page 179)

11. You feel extremely uneasy knowing you have a suicidal patient in your care. You worry that you'll miss signs that he'll try it again. What can you do?

a) Decide that if he's determined to kill himself, there's very little you can do about it anyway.

b) Have him transferred to a different team where a more experienced nurse can care for him.

c) Tell him about your fears and try to form a pact. Say: "I'm a little uneasy that you'll do something to hurt yourself. Promise me you'll call for help before you try something like that again."

d) Ask another nurse to help you with him. A high-risk patient like this needs more support than you can give alone, no matter how experienced you are.

12. Mr. Gerald Paterno, a 52-year-old diabetic, has been very quiet since his leg was amputated. One morning he confesses to you, "I've been thinking about death a lot lately. My life just won't be the same any more and there's no one who can help me." What do you do now?

a) Wait until Mr. Paterno seems less depressed. Then take steps to refer him for counselling.

b) Give him time to work out his problems by himself. You don't want to interfere with his personal life.

c) Remove mirrors, nail files, silverware and other potentially lethal items from his room. Show him where his call light is. Tell him to call you if he needs you.

d) Remove all dangerous items from his room and see that someone stays with him at all times. Take immediate steps to refer him for psychiatric help. Document everything.

13. During final exam week at college, 19-year-old Janice Wilson attempted suicide by slashing her wrists. While you're dressing her wounds after suturing, she says, "Please don't tell my parents about this." What should you say?

a) Say, "That's not up to me, Janice. The doctor will decide."

b) Say, "Of course I won't — not if you don't want me to."

c) Say, "Why? Are you ashamed?"

d) Say, "I can't promise that. Why don't you tell them yourself?"

14. Twenty-year-old Betty Lane was raped as she was leaving night school. Shortly after she's admitted to the E.D. where you work, you call her mother. When Betty's mother arrives, you explain what has happened and tell her she can see her daughter in a few minutes. She hesitates and tells you, "But I can't face her." What should you say?

a) Say, "She needs your support now more than ever."

b) Say, "You say you can't face your own daughter after what she's been through?"

c) Say, "Rape's an unpleasant thing. Would you like to discuss it with someone first?"

d) Say, "Then go in when you feel like it."

15. Jerry Grant, a 26-year-old shipping clerk, is admitted to the E.D. unconscious after collapsing at a nearby shopping mall. The ambulance driver can't tell you exactly what happened, but Mr. Grant's pulse rate is 60, his respiration rate is 12, and his temperature is 97° F. (36.1° C.). You note his skin's cold and clammy and that his pupils are dilated. Given these signs, which of the following conditions are likely:

a) Alcoholic intoxication

b) Diabetic acidosis

c) Barbiturate overdose

d) Traumatic head injury

e) Hypoglycemia

f) Epilepsy

16. One evening when you're on duty in the E.D., 30-year-old Donna Franklin comes in with her young daughter, Melissa. Donna's a nurse you occasionally work with. As you talk, she explains that 5-year-old Melissa may have dislocated her shoulder. When you ask how, Donna looks uncomfortable and says, "What's the difference? Right now, her shoulder needs attention." What should you do next?

a) Decide not to make an issue of it and concentrate on the injury.

b) Drop it for now, but resolve to talk to Donna alone the next time you're on duty together.

c) Suspect child abuse and look for injuries.

d) Ask Donna if she was present when Melissa got hurt.

e) Tell Donna that Melissa's injury suggests child abuse.

(Answers on page 179)

HELPING
HEALTH-CARE
PROFESSIONALS
IN CRISIS

"Coping with the physical and emotional needs of patients, day after day, causes tension. And mounting tension can turn your unit into a pressure cooker."

"Watch for danger signs that indicate your unit's stress level's too great. When that happens almost anything can trigger a crisis."

"Accepting your feelings is the first step toward easing your stress. If you're angry, jealous, or frustrated, acknowledge it."

"When you worry about burnout, talk about it. Sharing your feelings with other nurses helps, because they're in the best position to understand."

10
Coping with professional burnout

BY BARBARA F. MC VAN, RN

YOU'VE BEEN A DEDICATED NURSE. Until now your work's
been satisfying. Of course, the job's been rough at times but
you've survived. And most of the time you've been happy.
Now, for reasons you can't understand, you're uneasy. Your
job begins to frustrate you. You try coping in ways that've
worked in the past. You tell yourself to ignore your irritations
because they come with the job; you try to laugh them off,
or you complain to your family and friends.

But your dissatisfaction grows. Soon your usual coping
mechanisms don't help, so you try new ones: destructive
mechanisms like referring to patients by the name of their
disease; calling in sick when you're not; becoming cynical.

The circle is set. Now you don't like what you've become,
but you've lost sight of how the problem got started. Is there
any way out? Yes. For practical help, read this chapter. It'll
show you how to:
• identify and manage your immediate stress
• define possible causes and contributing factors
• find a solution that's right for you
• implement new, realistic goals
• evaluate the choice you've made.

Two sides of burnout

How do you picture the nurse who's in danger of burnout? Perhaps you think of the nurse who's become totally detached from her patients. No longer able to face her responsibilities, she starts avoiding them.

But what about the nurse who's become *overinvolved* with her patients? She's so preoccupied that she can't separate her professional life from her personal life. She works at a frenzied pace for as long as she can.

In both cases, the result's the same: professional burnout. And in both cases, the solution's the same: careful assessment and intervention.

Looking for symptoms

Are you in crisis? How can you tell? What symptoms do you look for? Assess yourself as you would a patient, using the same procedure you learned in Chapter 1. Ask yourself, am I behaving unusually? The following specific questions may help you answer.

Do you categorize or label your patients? For example, do you call anyone of them "a typical welfare patient" or "the lady with throat cancer," or simply, "Room 316"?

Have you become sarcastic or cynical? Do you say things like "The old man in 221 went off the edge last night. I thought he'd wake up every patient in the unit. It took half the night to calm things down."

Do you spend more time socializing with the staff than you should? When you chat with the other nurses, do you think "I really should be passing these medications" or "I really should be starting that retention enema"?

Do you concentrate on one part of your job and neglect others? For example, do other nurses complain that you're always doing in-depth teaching or spending a lot of time charting?

Do you feel you're not getting your co-workers' complete support? Do you ever say to yourself, "I'm the only one on this unit doing a good job"?

Do you feel professionally inadequate? Are your patients' needs overwhelming? Do you work through your lunch hour? Do you regularly stay late?

Do you unconsciously avoid your patients? Do you call in sick when you're depressed? Do you catch every bug that goes around?

Are your wishes unrealistic? For example, when you care for a dying patient, do you wish you could give him "some of your life"?

Have you answered "yes" to any of these questions? Chances are you have, if you've been honest with yourself. Of course, that doesn't necessarily mean you're a victim of professional burnout. But these symptoms may mean you're under great stress. Read the rest of this chapter to learn how to cope with that stress.

But suppose you've qualified your "yes" answers with these statements: "But I have a good reason for acting like that" or "In my case, it's different." Like all the above symptoms, your rationalization's a coping mechanism—an ineffective one.

Taking care of yourself

Accepting your feelings is the first step toward easing your stress. If you're angry, jealous, or frustrated, acknowledge it. Then you can take some positive actions to cope with these feelings. Begin by asking yourself, "How can I change things?"

To illustrate how this can help, consider Cindy Freeman, who works in the ICU. For several weeks she's been working extended shifts caring for the victims of a tragic school bus accident. She's desperate for a reprieve. Days off come irregularly and seem over before they've begun. Cindy needs relief from her immediate stress. What can she do?

Because Cindy's job revolves around helping others, thinking about her own problems seems selfish to her. To make matters worse, she knows the quality of her nursing care declines as her frustration and stress mount. She owes it to herself and her patients to confront her problem.

She has several immediate options. Perhaps she can trade a day off with another nurse to get two off in a row. Or maybe her supervisor can assign her to other patients for a while.

By relieving the most pressing stress, Cindy can begin identifying the larger problems creating her anxiety.

Ask yourself, "What's bothering me?" Narrow the field. Is the problem a personal one? For example:
- Do you like nursing?
- Are you prepared for what you encounter in your job?
- Are you in a specialty you like?
- Do you expect too much of yourself?

Maybe the problem's with your unit or hospital. For example:
- Are you working with poorly trained nurses?
- Does hospital policy hinder your work?
- Is your unit understaffed?
- Do you get credit for your good work?
- Does your supervisor listen when you have a complaint or need help?

Solving your problem

Your answers to these questions, or ones you've raised yourself, will help you decide what's wrong. Is your problem complex? One that involves everyone in the unit? If it is, read

How to get a transfer

After careful thought, you've decided to ask for a transfer from your unit. Here's how to get things moving:
- Put your request in writing. Specify the shift and unit you want. Then briefly list your reasons, keeping the tone positive. Make three copies and keep one for yourself.
- Tell the head nurse you're currently working with about your request and give her a copy of it. Maintain rapport with her, even though you plan to leave.
- Make an appointment to see the director of nursing (or whoever initiates transfers in your hospital) and give her your request personally. Explain exactly why you want to transfer: for example, you desire a broader background, or you're having trouble fitting into your current unit.
- Show the director of nursing you're serious about transferring by following up on your request in a few weeks.
- Don't expect to be transferred immediately. You may have to wait for an opening in another unit, or for your replacement to be found.

Burnout in specialty units

Because of the high stress level in ICUs, the nurses working in them are especially susceptible to burnout. But why? Doesn't the typical ICU nurse thrive under pressure?

Under most circumstances, yes. But when a patient's condition looks hopeless, even she can become overinvolved and lose her perspective. Imagining that better nursing care can save him, she pushes herself physically and emotionally. The result: burnout.

Another nurse who's distressed by the rapid turnover of patients may respond by refusing to get involved. But this, too, is a poor way to cope with the stress of ICU nursing. The more she succeeds in shielding herself from her patients, the less likely she is to assess their condition accurately.

Still another nurse may try to cope by hiding behind the ICU's vast array of machinery. She may get so involved monitoring and maintaining equipment that she begins ignoring the patient.

How can you combat the hazards of burnout if you're working in an ICU?
• Take your assigned breaks; don't work straight through your shift without one.
• Don't associate exclusively with the other ICU nurses. To make friends outside your unit, eat your meals with nurses who work on other floors.
• Find out if your hospital allows for rotation between the intensive care unit and other units that are less demanding.

No matter how well you work under pressure, ICU nursing can jeopardize your equilibrium. Don't let it. Use these practical tips to stay on top of your stress.

Chapter 11 in addition to this one. It will tell you how to deal with unit burnout.

Pinpoint your stress. Perhaps, like some nurses do, you feel stifled by doctors who treat you as a handmaiden. Or, like others, you "just don't like OB nursing." Identifying your major stress is an important step in relieving burnout.

Try to accept your predicament *temporarily*. Remember, you can't ignore a problem and work to solve it simultaneously. Try to be objective. What are your options? Remember, no problem is without a solution. Perhaps one of these will work for you:

• Solution 1—Continue your education. Doing so can increase your working knowledge and self-assurance. Consider Helen Jarrett, who works in an OB delivery room. As more patients demanded the right to try natural childbirth methods, Helen became increasingly distressed. When she realized her stress came from her unfamiliarity with these methods, she enrolled in a course that explained them. The program seemed so worthwhile that she asked the hospital to institute a similar one for other nurses interested in the new methods. Confident that she understands things better, Helen now offers her patients greater support.

Don't overlook courses in areas outside your unit's work. By increasing your awareness, they can help you develop greater self-discipline, and challenge you to seek new goals. What's more, you'll probably meet other nurses facing challenges similar to yours. Discovering their perspectives may help you revise and improve your own.

• Solution 2—Ask for a lateral transfer or a change of shift. Either may help you find greater job satisfaction. Frieda Turner tried one, after working in a medical unit of an oncology hospital for 4 years. Caring for so many terminally ill patients day after day began to depress her. Eventually she dreaded going to work and needed a change. When she realized why she was unhappy, she took a new look at her goals. Caring for a greater variety of patients was one of them. So Frieda transferred to the cancer screening unit where she saw over 50 new patients each day. Besides fulfilling a basic goal, the job developed her organizational skills and priority-setting abilities.

Important: Be sure your specific job assignment is the problem. If you're disillusioned with nursing in general, changing

"Watch for the nurse who copes with crisis by cutting herself off from others. She's a prime candidate for burnout."

NURSE'S GUIDE TO SELF-ASSESSMENT

What's the most effective way to prevent burnout from happening? Take a few moments to assess your professional and personal goals, your likes and dislikes, your personality, and job satisfaction.
Read the following questions carefully. Then write out your answers. They may help you better understand yourself.

SECTION 1—EXPLORING YOUR TEMPERAMENT
What things make you happy?

• Name two or three good experiences you've had recently.

_____
_____
_____

• What did they have in common?

_____
_____
_____

• When you're happy, how does that mood show itself in your behavior?

_____
_____
_____

What things upset you?

• Name a few upsetting situations that have happened to you recently.

_____
_____
_____

• What did they have in common?

_____
_____

• How do you deal with upsetting situations?

_____
_____
_____

Are any of the things that upset you part of your job?

• Are they part of your work or do they just occur unexpectedly?

_____

• Can you insure that the good things continue to happen?

_____

• Can you avoid the unpleasant things?

_____

SECTION 2—EXPLORING YOUR SELF-IMAGE
What activities do you enjoy?

• Why do you enjoy them? Because they make money? Relieve tension? Minimize boredom? Accomplish something? Challenge you? Provide you with opportunities to make new friends?

_____
_____

What activities do you hate?

• Why? Do they waste time? Cause you pain? Frustrate you? Bore you? Other reasons?

_____

Do you consider yourself solitary or outgoing by nature?

• When you do the things you enjoy, are you alone or with others?

• When you do the things you hate, are you alone or with others?

_____

What type of people do you usually associate with?

• Are they loners or socializers?

_____

• What do they have in common?

_____

• In what ways are they different?

_____

Where do you fit in?

• In what ways are you like your friends? What traits do they have that you wish you had?

_____
_____
_____

- In what ways are you different?

_____

_____

_____

What are your limitations?

- Are they physical? Mental? Emotional?

_____

- How does that knowledge affect you? Do you accept your limitations? Try to overcome them? Or become frustrated by them?

_____

_____

_____

SECTION 3—EXPLORING YOUR PERSONAL AND PROFESSIONAL GOALS
How do you work in relation to others?

- Are you a leader?

_____

- Do you follow instructions well?

_____

- Do you seek out extra responsibilities?

_____

- Do you feel you have unrecognized or untapped talents?

_____

What motivates you? What are your supports?

- Family and friends?

_____

_____

- Religious or ethical beliefs?

- Personal challenge? Self-improvement?

_____

When are you at your best?

- Do you work best under pressure? Or at your own speed?

_____

_____

- Are you at your best in the morning? Afternoon? Or evening?

_____

_____

How do you feel about your job? List the following in order of importance to you:

- I'm challenged by my work.   ☐

- I'm at ease with my work and enjoy myself.   ☐

- I get along well with my co-workers and supervisors.   ☐

- It's rewarding work.   ☐

- I feel economically secure.   ☐

- It furthers my goals.   ☐

How many are true about your current position?

_____

_____

Now that you've finished the test, consider your answers. Together they can give you a better understanding of your temperament, self-image, and personal and professional goals. Explore these possibilities:
- If your answers reveal a deep interest in helping others, keep that interest in mind, particularly if you're offered a promotion which would take you away from direct patient care.
- If your answers show a strong desire to control things, that may explain why you can't get along with some doctors while others can. Sometimes just knowing *why* you're angry helps you deal with it.
- Maybe your answers tell you something you've avoided facing before this: that your job's benefits don't outweigh its shortcomings. When that happens, consider transferring. Then, if you do take another job, repeat this test in two or three months to see whether the move fulfilled your expectations.
- Perhaps your answers reveal you don't feel committed to anything. Instead of having clear-cut goals to work for, you drift about aimlessly and never accomplish anything. Don't assume this is a character flaw. Perhaps you're in the wrong job. Weigh your interests. Look for the job that's right for you.
     Remember, the conclusions you draw from this test will help you understand what's important to you. That, in turn, will help you answer the question: "What are my nursing goals?" Until you know what you really want and need, and are willing to act on those needs, you'll always face the possibility of burnout.

Learning your limitations

Suppose your self-assessment indicates your present position's leading you to professional burnout. Or maybe you feel that you just can't satisfy your goals by staying where you are. So you decide to transfer to a position with fewer responsibilities or less pressure. Are you concerned that others may think your new position's a step down? Are you unsure you've made the right move?

Here are some suggestions to help you cope with the change:

• List the reasons for your decision to change jobs. Make them clear so you can understand and accept each one. For tips on how to arrange a transfer, see page 155.

• Before you do make a position change, be certain your present duties are the real problem. If something else is bothering you, changing positions isn't the answer.

• Set realistic goals to achieve in your new position. Concentrate on them.

• If possible, take a short vacation so you can start anew when you return.

• Offer positive comments about the position you've left and the people you worked with. Negative comments may dampen another nurse's desire to attain that position someday. They also reflect negatively on you.

• Don't criticize your new co-workers. Otherwise, you may give the impression you've "stepped down" to teach them how to do their jobs. Do offer your help freely whenever you're asked.

• Feel good about your decision. Remember, you've taken a positive step. Accepting yourself, limitations and all, is an act of courage.

responsibilities won't help.

• Solution 3—Find a new, positive way to let off steam. Consider Bea Gillam who goes home to her three teenage children after a day in the E.D. At the end of her workday she feels like she's trading one crisis environment for another. She loves her family but needs time for herself. So, she decides to try jogging after work. Running a couple of miles each evening is just enough to help her unwind. Now when she leaves work, she's eager to return home.

If strenuous physical activity doesn't appeal to you, try yoga or meditation, or take lessons on a musical instrument. Some people take a nap or relax in the tub before dinner. Choose what's best for you. But avoid destructive coping habits. For example, drinking excessively will only add to your stress.

• Solution 4—Organize a group to discuss job frustrations. For example, consider the team caring for 84-year-old Mrs. Callahan, a "difficult" patient. Although she's recovering satisfactorily from a fractured hip, she refuses to believe it. She picks at her meals, throws food on the floor and insults the nurses. Every time one of them enters the room, Mrs. Callahan lists her complaints.

The unit has a meeting. They ask, "How can we deal with this patient and still maintain our cool?" They decide to share and rotate care responsibility. They adopt a uniform reaction to her requests and actions. By creating a stable environment for Mrs. Callahan, they can care for her more effectively.

This unit's good working relationship offers its members mutual support. Remember: Sharing your feelings with other nurses helps, because they're in the best position to understand. When you worry about burnout, talk about it. Don't let your pride create unnecessary barriers. These barriers, by themselves, cause more burnout than patient care stress.

• Solution 5—Give up unrealistic goals and replace them with realistic ones. Consider Jenny Howard, a new graduate. Although one of her patients is dying from lung cancer, Jenny's sure she can rehabilitate him. When he doesn't respond, she becomes increasingly frustrated. She's not sure she's cut out to be a nurse. Eventually the man she's caring for says: "Young lady, I know I'm dying. I wish you wouldn't pretend otherwise." Only then does Jenny realize what she's been doing. After discussing it, Jenny and her patient face his impending death together.

"Is your present position catapulting you into professional burn-out? Consider stepping down to a job with fewer responsibilities. Accepting your limitations is always a positive act."

• Solution 6—Deal with your problems innovatively instead of combatively. Consider head nurse Anne Kelly's predicament, when Beatrice Lawson returns to nursing after a 15-year retirement. Although Beatrice has taken a refresher course, Anne notices she's forgotten how to do some of the simpler procedures. However, Anne's attempts to help or correct her bring only resentment. One day when Anne observes Beatrice's suctioning technique, she sees how to resolve the problem. She calls a general team conference to focus on good suctioning. To Anne's relief, Beatrice corrects her technique that same day.

Evaluating your choice
Now that you've discovered some practical ways to reverse burnout, pick one and try it. But don't forget to evaluate your choice to see if it's the right one.

Suppose it doesn't work? Consider the following case to help determine your next move.

After several years as a charge nurse, Ellen Pughe begins suffering burnout symptoms. Assessing her problem, she decides she needs a more challenging position, one in which she can upgrade the quality of patient care. So she accepts a new position as assistant head nurse on a surgical unit. But instead of feeling better about her work, she becomes more dissatisfied. In time, she realizes that it wasn't more responsibility she was seeking; it was closer contact with her patients. The new job doesn't work out. She requests a transfer to a team of patient-teaching specialists. Now working in-depth with ostomy patients, Ellen feels more satisfied.

Facing the challenge
You may face burnout many times in your career. And when you do, you may have trouble identifying its cause on the first try. But keep trying. Recognize burnout as an opportunity to reevaluate your nursing goals and grow. Burnout won't destroy your career unless you let it. By coping with it effectively the first time it occurs, you'll be better able to deal with it later—in yourself and your co-workers.

Recognizing and dealing with unit crisis

BY THERESA CROUSHORE, RN

ONE DAY YOU ARRIVE for work and notice a change in your unit's atmosphere. You ask, "What's up?" and find out the head nurse was called to the supervisor's office the day before. Now she's irritable and grumpy but won't explain why. As the day wears on, her uneasiness spreads like a contagious disease. Co-workers become curt with one another. Soon patient care and your unit's working relationship with others is affected. Your unit's in crisis.

What triggered the crisis? How can you restore your unit's equilibrium? Do the crisis assessment and intervention techniques you learned in Chapters 1 and 2 apply to a unit? Read this chapter and find out. It'll tell you how to:
• Recognize mounting unit stress
• Identify and deal with threats most likely to trigger crisis
• Assess balancing factors
• Strengthen unit equilibrium to avoid future crises.

The pressure-cooker unit
As you know, being a nurse isn't easy. Coping with the physical and emotional needs of patients, day after day, causes tension and makes any unit susceptible to crisis. Unexpected or up-

setting events can't be avoided. But you can keep them from turning your unit into a pressure cooker. Watch for these danger signs:

• *Gossiping and quarreling.* Do you spend a lot of time discussing the activities and shortcomings of other nurses? Do you speak to each other with "knowing glances"? Do you bicker with one another or with other units?

• *Cliques.* Has your unit split into little groups? Do some of you share information and in-jokes but exclude others? Do all of you consciously avoid talking to certain other units or departments?

• *Scapegoating.* When a patient care problem surfaces, do you and others automatically blame a co-worker? For example, do you say, "Well, it's not hard to guess who made that blunder."

• *Increased absence.* Do you or your co-workers get sick a lot? Are those in your unit consistently late for work? Does anyone spend too much time socializing?

• *Lack of cooperation.* Does your unit have problems carrying out care plans? Do any of you fail to follow agreed-on routines? Does your unit find it increasingly difficult to get along with other units? Do most of you resent changes in staff or responsibilities?

• *Manipulation.* Does any patient consistently get his own way no matter how it affects the others? Do any of them play one nurse against another? Conversely, do any nurses regularly use patients to get at other nurses?

• *Patient complaints.* Are most patients dissatisfied with the care they receive in your unit? Do patients repeatedly complain you've failed to provide them with information they've requested? Do any patients ask not to be sent to your unit?

• *Over-involvement.* Do any of you become so obsessed with one patient's problems that you neglect other duties? Or do any of you so identify with a patient that you can't care for him properly?

• *Detachment.* Do any of you seem to ignore patients with particular illnesses or problems? Do you "forget" to care for some patients?

Perhaps you're saying to yourself: "No unit is without some of these signs." That's true. But when you notice even one, work hard to relieve the tension. Then the events that normally trigger crisis in a pressure-cooker unit will be taken in stride.

HOW TO COMMUNICATE WITH A CO-WORKER

What's the best way to help a co-worker in burnout? Talk with her about it. If a nurse in your unit seems out of sorts or preoccupied, ask her about it diplomatically. Show concern and a willingness to listen by saying something like, "Charting's taking up a lot of your time lately. Is there anything I can do to help?"

She may reject your offer. If so, don't take her rebuff personally. Your anger will only add to unit stress. If you feel her problem's affecting patient care, talk to your superior about it.

On the other hand, she may respond to your offer by telling you what's bothering her. Discuss the problem with her. Assess her as you would a patient:
● Does she perceive the problem realistically? If not, share your views with her. Maybe your perspective will help her clarify the problem in her mind.

● How is she coping? Does she know all the alternatives — like those discussed in Chapter 10—that are open to her?
● Find out what her supports are. In this instance, you yourself can be of immediate help. Listen to her attentively. Respect her confidence and trust in you.

Remember, your show of concern may help not only to relieve one co-worker's stress, but to prevent unit crisis as well.

Beware of the last straw

Suppose you see your unit's stress level mounting with no relief in sight. Stay alert. Anything can trigger a crisis. But what events are especially risky? A co-worker's extreme anxiety is one. To illustrate, think back to the beginning of the chapter. What happened in that unit that caused it to go into crisis? How did you discover it?

First you determined that the head nurse's anxiety triggered your unit's crisis. Like something in the wind, that anxiety floated through the unit affecting everyone, yet no one seemed to understand what was happening. So you confronted the head nurse with the situation, and she told you she was upset because the hospital wanted to transfer her to another unit. Later that day, however, the crisis passed. The administration decided to leave the head nurse where she was and the unit learned the whole story.

Free-floating anxiety is something that can surface anytime, adding an extra burden of stress to an already tense unit. Other events that may trigger a crisis in a pressure-cooker unit are:
Loss. Remember the last time one of your unit members resigned, transferred, or was fired? How did you and the others

Fitting into a new unit

Adjusting to a new unit can be stressful, no matter how long you've been a nurse. To make it easier, follow these suggestions:
• Find out what the unit's nursing goals are. For example, which aspect of patient care has top priority? How important is preop teaching? Whatever your new unit's goals, try to adjust to them.
• Take time to read the policy and procedure books for your unit.
• Understand your responsibilities and those of your co-workers. Do they match actual staff performance? Find out exactly what's expected of you.
• Stick to the rules until you learn how flexible they are. If the lunch break's 30 minutes, take 30 minutes—no more, no less. Later, you may find that longer lunch breaks are permitted, depending on that day's workload.
• Assess the unit's formality. If everyone calls the head nurse Miss Wilson, do the same, even if she's 10 years your junior. Or if everyone else calls her Carol, ask if you can too.
• If you're unfamiliar with the hospital and its procedures, admit it. Don't be embarrassed to ask. If you don't know how to get around the building, request a tour. If you don't understand the phone system, ask how it works.
• Make an effort to know the people you work with. Share information about yourself with them, and encourage them to do the same.

react? Chances are, most everyone reacted differently. Those particularly close to the departing nurse may have been depressed. Others less close may not have been affected by her departure. Still others who perhaps didn't get along with her were glad she left. Or perhaps they felt guilty because they hadn't tried harder to work well with her.

Do varying perceptions like these hurt patient care? They may. Fairly soon after the triggering event, you'll know whether the unit can adjust to the loss. If it can't, the loss may cause hard feelings. For example, if you were friendly with the departed nurse, you may believe others made it too difficult for her to stay. Rancor of this sort eats away at everyone's ability to work well together. If you see it developing in yourself or others, talk it over with the nurses, the head nurse, or the unit supervisor. (For tips on what to say, see page 170.)

Some other losses you and others in your unit will react to are these:
• when a patient you're close to dies
• when some of your responsibilities are taken away from you
• when your unit's temporarily closed.

Threat of change. Can your unit adjust to change? What would happen to your unit if the hospital made a substantial policy revision? Consider the unit that's always used a narrative method of charting. When the hospital switches to the newer problem-oriented method, some of your co-workers aren't sure they can adjust. They ask themselves: "How can I remember all this?" "What if I can't?" "Will I lose my job?"

When unit efficiency is affected, the quality of patient care deteriorates. Sometimes unit or team discussions about the new rules can keep this from happening. Reassurance from superiors can be particularly helpful during times of change. If you see complications developing, tell your supervisor about them.

Threat of change can come in many forms. Has a new nurse ever disrupted the routine of your unit? Or do you know a head nurse who confronted resentment when she first took over? Learn resilience. Remember, the unit flexible enough to change minimizes its chances of crisis.

Catastrophe. Has your unit ever been faced with an emotionally overwhelming event? How did it react? For example, suppose you're working in an ICU that's stunned by this tragic

"Having trouble fitting into a new unit? Don't be embarrassed to ask questions. Find out exactly what's expected of you."

news: The seriously injured child you're treating after a car accident is the daughter of a co-worker. Not only is that crushing moment difficult to deal with, but so are the months of intensive care that come afterwards. You all cope differently. Some nurses are numbed by the event and have trouble concentrating on their work. Others throw themselves into their jobs and become overly efficient. Still others try to detach themselves from the event, acting as if it never happened. Whether any of you recognize it or not, your concern for the child and her mother has diverted your energies and affected your patient care. Once you're aware what's happening, you can help pull the unit out of crisis.

Sometimes catastrophic situations unify, instead of divide a unit. Suppose you're in a hospital that catches fire. As you work with the other nurses to battle this common enemy, you look at each other in a new way. Old conflicts disappear as the shattering event forces all of you together for support and comfort. Such a catastrophe, while regrettable in itself, may ultimately benefit your distressed unit.

Conflicting values. What happens when you disagree with someone over a moral or ethical point? Does it affect how you relate to him? Consider the alcoholic patient. How you and unit members perceive his problem will affect how you treat him. For example, contempt may cause some nurses to neglect him. Pity may cause some to fuss over him too much. When your attitudes clash with those of others, the entire unit may become disrupted.

Now consider what might happen if you found out one of your married co-workers was having an affair with a doctor. You may disregard it by saying, "It's none of my business." But if you disapprove, your attitude may color and perhaps damage your working relationship with that nurse. Don't make hasty judgments. Try to be objective. Above all, watch the problems your attitudes cause.

Personality conflicts. Have you ever found it impossible to get along with someone? Has the personality of one nurse thrown your entire unit in crisis? For example, consider the conflicts caused by a likeable but poorly trained nurse. She's an obvious threat to patient care, but who wants to call attention to her faults? So, if you're like most nurses, you cope by denial; you simply ignore her inadequacies. Then, when patient care is affected and something regrettable happens, you and the other nurses feel guilty. With hindsight you say, "We should've corrected the situation earlier." Sometimes resentment is the response. Those of you who end up doing her work stew over it until you finally explode. Your overreaction diverts attention from the main problem—the poorly trained nurse—and leaves your unit no closer to a solution.

The burned-out nurse can cause similar problems. Her indifference to work can be infectious and demoralizing. But you can help her if you know how to recognize and cope with individual burnout. For specific tips on this problem, see Chapter 10.

An exceptionally competent nurse can also put a unit in crisis. Depending on her attitude, she can create feelings of inadequacy, resentment, or jealousy in fellow nurses. Resist comparing yourself with her. Recognize that your responsibility ends with being the best *you* can be. Don't let one nurse set the standards for all. If you do, your unit's ability to work together will be destroyed. *Good nursing is patient care done competently, not competitively.*

Understaffing. How does your unit react when it's short-handed? Do unit members resist assuming more responsibilities? Did your hospital ever cut back the number of nurses in your unit? If you're like most nurses, your first reaction is to gripe about the situation: "It'd sure be nice if the administration would help us once in a while." Then, when your unit simply can't accomplish all it used to, you begin cutting back on patient care. But that's risky. If you aren't careful, you may eliminate something crucial. Make the unit supervisor aware of this threat so she can help trim unit tasks and set priorities. Then the unit won't be overburdened and can continue providing good patient care.

Everyday balancing factors

Of course, the triggering events I've just talked about are less likely to cause crisis in your unit if you deal beforehand with underlying stress. How can you tell if your unit's balancing factors are sound? What can you do to relieve your everyday tension? Knowing your job and feeling secure in it can really help. To determine how you and the other nurses in your unit feel about your jobs, ask these questions:

• What are your responsibilities? How do they relate to the responsibilities of other unit members?

How to talk with your supervisor

How do you tell your supervisor that you think your unit's in crisis?

First, for privacy's sake, request an appointment. If you think you know what's causing the problem, cite examples to support your case. But if you have only a feeling something's wrong, make that plain. Say something like, "I sense our unit's under a lot of stress. I don't exactly know why, but we're more defensive, more jumpy than usual. It makes me uncomfortable."

Follow these additional guidelines:
• Don't imply that your unit's in trouble because of her lack of leadership. That'll only alienate your supervisor.
• Don't discuss the problem with anyone else. To do so may only create further tension.
• Don't suggest solutions until you've given the supervisor a chance to consider what you've said.

Perhaps your supervisor's sensed that tension too. Listen to her views and support her plan of action.

What if she thinks you're overreacting? Consider that possibility. But if after a week or so nothing's changed, speak to her again. If she still refuses to recognize the problem, tell her you want to bring it to her supervisor's attention.

• Who do you report to? Is there a lack of leadership in your unit? Is there conflicting leadership?
• What are the hospital policies regarding your position? Does everyone know them? Does everyone follow them?
• What are the hospital's policies and procedures regarding patient care? Does everyone know them? Does everyone follow them?
• What are your unit's goals? Does everyone understand them? Does everyone agree with them?
• Who can you discuss problems with in your unit? What can you talk about freely?

Avoiding future crisis

Can you answer the above questions without hesitation? If you can't, you're not alone. What can you do about it? Go to your unit supervisor. She can answer some of your questions. We've included some suggestions on the next few pages to help her deal with the more complicated problems.

In the meantime, try to get better acquainted with the other nurses in your unit. Strive to understand their point of view. Free and open discussion of problems or disagreements will make working together easier. And when teamwork becomes easier, crisis becomes less likely.

How the supervisor can help

Suppose *you're* the supervisor, head nurse, or team leader on a floor that shows signs of mounting stress. What can you do to relieve underlying stress? Here are some guidelines to help you:

Know your staff. Learn how each will respond to change, to challenge, to thwarted goals. How can you find out? Talk to each one personally. Let her steer the conversation. As you listen, ask yourself these questions:
• What's her self-image?
• What are her strengths and weaknesses?
• What characteristics does she admire in her co-workers?
• Is she a leader or a follower? How does she treat others?
• What's her work area like? Does it reflect her personality?
Use your knowledge of each nurse to gain her cooperation. When you present new ideas to her, try to relate them to her self-image. For example, say something like: "Mary, everyone looks up to you. When you started ordering all the supplies

"When you sense your unit's under a lot of stress, discuss it with your supervisor. Don't gossip about the problem with nurses from other units."

you'd need for a shift at one time, others followed your lead. Now we'll be changing to SOAP charting. Your cooperation will make it easier for the rest."

Communicate on their level. When you assign work or discuss changes, don't explain things they already understand. Tailor your instructions to your listeners' professional level.

Give each nurse room to grow. Respect individual opinions and encourage new ideas. Allow each to try out new roles by delegating some of your responsibilities. For example, if you're in charge of scheduling, assign that job to one of the staff nurses while you're on vacation. If she copes well, make sure she gets the credit. Keep stressing her strengths.

Let your staff know what's expected of them. Enforce the guidelines listed in the hospital's policy and procedure manuals. Make job descriptions meaningful by being specific. Don't just write, "Give complete bedside care." Instead, list all the nurse's responsibilities. Write: "Order supplies needed to treat all patients in your care."

Establish unit goals. First, encourage everyone to participate. Then, call a staff meeting to list the unit's short- and long-term goals. Make the goals measurable. Don't be vague. For example, don't set "Improving patient care" as a long-term goal. Instead write something like "Provide the quality of care needed to decrease these postop complications: infections, atelectasis, and phlebitis."

Your short-term goals should help you achieve the long-term ones. For example, to reduce postop complications, you may decide on this short-term goal: "Change I.V. sites every 48 hours on the 7 to 3 shift." Make sure everyone finds the goals acceptable, so they'll work toward them.

Use continuing education as a way to achieve unit goals. If possible, include staff nurses as teachers. Is one of your nurses particularly good at performing venipunctures? Let her share her ideas. Then suggest that she continue offering tips while she works.

Keep everyone goal-oriented by posting unit goals on a bulletin board. Remember to congratulate the staff as each short-term goal is achieved.

Set a good example. You can influence how your staff functions by setting and maintaining high professional standards for yourself.

Don't let your staff feel they're doing most of the work.

Share in their responsibilities. Let them know you're ready and willing to answer questions or demonstrate techniques. If you anticipate being tied up, tell them when you'll be available again.

Encourage an atmosphere of positivism. Help your staff members feel enthusiastic about their work by showing enthusiasm yourself.

Know how to manage problems that create additional stress. To help, the rest of this chapter includes guidelines you can use for specific situations.

How to initiate a change

Even a minor change can meet with resistance if feelings of security are threatened. No nurse welcomes a change if she's happy with the status quo.

Abrupt changes are usually the hardest to deal with. In such circumstances, be decisive. State the new instructions simply and clearly. Give the reasons why the change was made, if you know them. For example, say: "Starting today, we can no longer park in the north parking lot, because the light's inadequate."

In most cases, you'll have time to prepare your staff for a change. When you do, follow these guidelines:

• Encourage a positive attitude toward change. Stress the need to welcome constructive changes as a way to improve patient care. When you sense certain routines need changing, alert your staff. Say: "There must be a better way of doing this. If any of you can think of one, let me know."

• Let them help. Ask questions to get staff input, and show enthusiasm when someone makes a constructive suggestion. Give credit to the originator of every good idea. Involve that person when you initiate the change.

• Don't rush things. Let staff members get accustomed to changes gradually. For example, suppose hospital policy states that you must switch to the new problem-oriented method of charting (SOAP). Teach your staff how to write SOAP progress notes before you ask them to change the style of the care plans.

• Be sure the staff understands your new instructions exactly. Make the reasons for change relevant to each nurse. If the change involves new equipment, teach her how to use it. Make sure you answer her questions.

Initiating a policy change
When you talk about any policy change with your supervisor, be able to:
• Discuss current policy intelligently.
• List your reasons for requesting the change.
• Explain how the change will improve patient care and make your unit work more efficiently.
• Defend your proposal rationally and calmly. Accept reasonable changes others may suggest.

Clearing the air

Has a new group of medical students, interns, or residents arrived on your floor? Getting adjusted to these new health-care professionals may be all your unit needs to throw it into crisis.

For example, suppose one of the new interns takes the attitude, "Don't tell me what to do," when a nurse makes a constructive suggestion. The hostility that's sure to build up will add to the unit's already high stress level.

How can you help?
• First, talk to your head nurse about setting up a group meeting with the medical staff. Talking things over will help clear the air.
• Don't let anyone go into the meeting like they're entering a battleground. To be truly therapeutic, a group meeting should be a discussion between mature adults, not a confrontation between doctors and nurses.
• Be candid and honest about your concerns. If a new resident acts condescending to you, admit you're upset. Start by saying something like, "You treat me as if I didn't know anything. But I think we can work together as a team to help the patients."
• Expect positive results from the meeting, but don't expect to accomplish miracles in one session. If the stress level in your unit's extremely high, you may want to start a program of weekly group sessions.

• Discourage negative thinking about the change, once it's in effect. If one of your staff says, "I don't know why they changed that procedure. I was happy with the old way," don't say, "So was I." Instead say, "I'm sure we'll see the benefits soon." Don't let complaining become an acceptable way of coping for your staff.

How to deal with a problem staff member

Suppose you sense your unit's tension stems from a personality conflict or someone's professional shortcomings? How can you pinpoint the source of the conflict? What can you do about it?

Don't assume you know who's causing the problem. Find out by listening to your staff and the patients on your floor. You may hear complaints about one particular nurse or nurse's aide. For example, the staff may tell you she's inattentive to details. And a patient may say, "Last night, the nurse with the blonde hair let me get out of bed. Why won't you?"

Once you've identified the problem, face it squarely. Use these guidelines to talk to the troublesome staff member:
• First, make a mental note of her good points. Plan what you're going to say so you can refer to her strengths, as well as her weaknesses.
• Schedule your conference for a time that doesn't interfere with other responsibilities. Then keep it private. Don't publicize a staff member's problems.
• When you meet, state the problem exactly as you see it, without getting angry. Be direct. Say something like: "Jenny, you're not following the patient care plans as carefully as you should." Don't wait for her to bring up the subject. She may not know why you're displeased.
• Direct your criticism at her actions, not at her character. *Never* use sarcasm.
• Encourage her to tell you how she sees the problem. Then try to understand her point of view.
• Tell her you want to work out a solution together. Explore her needs and try to accommodate them. For example, does she think she'd work better on another shift? Perhaps you can get her reassigned.
• Suggest ways she can improve. When you make suggestions, be specific. Make sure she understands and can follow them. But don't bombard her with too many things at one

time. Discuss her most pressing problems at your first meeting. If she improves in those areas, you can tackle her other problems later. Show confidence in her ability to change.

• Indicate exactly how long you'll wait for her to improve. Don't say: "I want to see a change in your attention to details soon." Say: "I want to see a change in your attention to details within 3 weeks." *Important:* After the conference, document what you've discussed in a confidential report and file it. You may need it later to substantiate what's been said.

• Give her time to work through her feelings. If she wants to discuss the matter with others, don't discourage her. She may need the support of her family, friends, or co-workers.

• Take care how much work you assign her. Don't burden her with additional responsibilities at a time she's working on her own problems.

• Meet again, when you're sure she's had enough time to adjust to your expectations. Discuss her progress, if any, and let her know where she stands. Be generous with your praise. Even a slight improvement deserves some recognition.

How to deal with the loss of a staff member
When someone leaves your unit, for whatever reason, you and your staff may feel the loss. The way you manage the situation may determine whether or not a unit crisis follows.

• *If a staff member resigns.* Give her co-workers time to say good-bye. If the workload permits, allow them to take longer lunch breaks. Be sensitive to the needs of those under you. Remember they're people, not just professionals.

• *If a staff member gets transferred.* Co-workers sometimes stay friendly with a nurse who transfers to another unit. Make sure visiting between floors doesn't become a problem. However, arrange it so they can eat together if they wish. Encourage the nurse's replacement to take part, too.

• *If a staff member's fired.* When you must fire someone, let her leave right away. If you can't, try to move her to another shift or floor until she can go. Otherwise, the other nurses may feel frustrated and guilt-ridden in her presence.

• *If a staff member dies.* Expect normal grief reactions from yourself and the staff. Make it possible for co-workers to attend the funeral, even if you must get extra help. Encourage staff members to express their feelings freely. Don't criticize anyone who doesn't react the way you'd expect. A grieving person's actions don't always show how she feels inside.

How to minimize the effects of understaffing

When your unit's short-staffed, you're all going to have a heavier workload. To get things done and prevent discouragement, try these helpful time-management techniques.

• Make realistic assignments. Start by considering how much care each incoming patient may need. Then ask the admissions office to make sure one team doesn't get all the difficult patients.

• Continue assigning low-priority jobs. For example, don't let jobs like checking supplies be neglected. They provide a release from more stressful responsibilities and keep the unit organized and efficient.

• Check priorities. Ask each nurse to list her responsibilities in the order of their importance. Make sure she's not including tasks she could delegate to a nurse's aide, family member, or the patient. Then hold her responsible for doing all she's listed.

• Ask for volunteer help. If the work gets too hectic, call in assistance for the easier but essential unit tasks.

How to introduce a new staff member into the unit

If you're not careful, a new staff member can seriously disrupt your unit. Why? Because the introduction of one new personality can change the way all the nurses interact with each other.

To minimize stress, follow the general guidelines we've already discussed for initiating change. Then try these tips:

• Give your staff a chance to meet their new co-worker before she starts. Tell them when she'll begin work.

• When she comes, give her a meaningful job description and explain her responsibilities. Describe in detail the unit's goals, policies, and procedures.

• Assign another nurse to work with her for at least a week. Having a "buddy" may hasten her acceptance into the unit.

Staying cool

Of course, problems like these don't always throw a unit in crisis. But they can increase the stress level to alarming proportions. No matter what position you hold in your unit, use the guidelines we've discussed in this chapter to prevent crisis. Learn how to work with stress, not struggle against it.

SKILLCHECK 3

I. Consider each of the following stories. Then assess each nurse. Do you think any of them is headed for professional burnout?

a) Alice Samuels has started singing with a jazz band in her free time. When she's not on duty at the hospital, she spends most of her time rehearsing or performing. She's always loved music and is thrilled at her new success as a performer. However, sometimes her love for music and her love for nursing conflict. This happens when she has to juggle her nursing hours to accommodate an engagement with the band.

b) Twenty-year-old Martha Bannister firmly believes that a nurse has special obligations to her patients. Because of this, she makes a great effort to become personally acquainted with each of them. Whenever she can spare a moment, she listens to their problems and encourages them to confide even more. Sometimes she stays overtime or works through lunch to give a distressed patient extra support. Martha's patients are always talking about her kind ways. Sometimes they even keep in touch with her after they're discharged.

c) Marie Donovan is a highly competent 22-year-old nurse, who trained at a large metropolitan hospital. When her family moves to a rural area, she starts working for a much smaller hospital that serves an entire county. To her dismay, she soon discovers that it's woefully understaffed and underfunded. Because all the nurses are overworked, their morale is low. What's more, patient care is barely adequate, measured by her high standards. Because of this, she seriously considers returning to her city job. However, Marie's nursing supervisor convinces her that the hospital needs nurses like Marie. She's receptive to Marie's suggestions on improving patient care and says she'll give Marie more responsibility. Encouraged by her supervisor's attitude, Marie decides to give her new job another try.

2. For 3 years you've worked on a medical/surgical floor with a competent nurse named Sarah Wales. You know that she's an exceptionally good nurse, who is always sensitive to her patients' needs. Until recently she's always been punctual and available when you've needed her. Now you notice that she's frequently late for work, but you let it pass without saying anything. One day a surprising incident oc-

curs. One of Sarah's more difficult patients, an elderly woman on complete bedrest, calls for help. Because Sarah can't be found, you answer the call. When you do, you find the patient stumbling around her room, looking for the bathroom. She's so confused and combative that you have to call another nurse to help you restrain her. After you've finally calmed the patient, you look again for Sarah. When you finally find her, she says "What do you want?" You detect alcohol on Sarah's breath. What do you do next?

a) Ask Sarah if she's been drinking.
b) Forget the incident and let Sarah cope with her own problems.
c) Explain what had happened to Sarah's patient, ignoring your suspicions that Sarah may have been drinking.
d) Go to your supervisor immediately, and tell her that Sarah has a drinking problem.
e) Avoid confronting Sarah until you can find a private place to talk. Then, ask her what you can do to help her.
f) Tell Sarah she's an alcoholic, and insist she call Alcoholics Anonymous.

3. Which of the following behaviors suggests you may be suffering from professional burnout?
a) You start concentrating exclusively on one part of your job.
b) You start categorizing your patients.
c) You maintain a professional distance between you and your patients.
d) You socialize with your co-workers.
e) You regularly work long hours overtime.

4. Which of the following statements are true and which are false?
a) The unit that runs with clocklike efficiency can always avoid the stressful events that sometimes trigger a crisis.
b) Every unit shows some signs of tension.
c) The first sign of professional burnout in a nurse is usually complete indifference to her patients.
d) Encouraging competition between nurses is a good way to meet unit goals.
e) The best units in any hospital are those in which every nurse is a born leader.
f) The nurse who thinks about her own needs while she's on duty is too selfish to be a good nurse.

(Answers on page 181)

SKILLCHECK ANSWERS

SKILLCHECK ANSWERS—SECTION 1 (page 39)

Situation 1

a) A child's unlikely to experience a crisis. This statement is false. A child's as vulnerable to crisis as anyone else, including the nurse who's skillful at crisis intervention. Although crisis can occur at any time in life, it's most likely to occur at a maturational point. Also, remember that a triggering factor always precedes a crisis.

Situation 2

e) A patient in crisis may have any of these reactions. He may cope successfully with no intervention. But he also may adopt inappropriate coping mechanisms by denying the severity of the problem or even ignoring it altogether.

Situation 3

f) Any of these interventions may be appropriate, depending on your assessment of the patient's stress level. Involving other professionals and family members in the intervention will strengthen the patient's support system. If he's violent or combative, a tranquilizer is an effective short-term intervention, provided the doctor orders it.

Situation 4

e) For a patient who's already under stress, a transfer or postponement may be just enough to trigger a crisis. An event that happened more than two weeks ago, even something as traumatic as a death in the family, isn't likely to trigger a crisis.

Situation 5

b) Encourage her to tell you what's wrong. Although you assume she's upset about the diagnostic tests, she may really be more worried about a domestic problem. If she does indicate that she wants to discuss the tests with you, don't avoid the subject. But beware of overwhelming her with all you know about complicated or painful procedures. If she has specific, detailed questions, tell her you'll ask the doctor to answer them. Then follow through.

Situation 6

a) To determine if Mr. Barrow's in crisis, you assess his balancing factors. You note that he has his wife's full support. He'll also be able to continue playing golf. Although he has doubts that he can adjust to his new diet and exercise schedule, you know he has two strong balancing factors present. Considering all the evidence, you don't think Mr. Barrow is threatened by crisis.

b) Assessing Lorry Barnhart's balancing factors, you observe she's extremely upset by her impending surgery, much more than most patients you've cared for. Even her husband, who's her strongest support, seems uncertain about how he'll react later. Although he tries to reassure her, his obvious anxiety indicates he's unsettled. You also realize that Ms. Barnhart's professional swimming career will suffer a serious setback until she rebuilds her arm and chest muscles. This challenge adds to her already high stress level. Considering your findings, you think Ms. Barnhart's facing crisis.

c) You assess Mark Thomas's balancing factors. Obviously, he fails to perceive his father's true situation realistically. But he does seem happy and well adjusted at school, judging by conversations you've heard. However, from your limited contact with him, you can't tell how he copes with stress or how much he relies on his father's support and presence. With the information you have available at that time, you're unsure whether or not Mark faces crisis. You continue to assess his stress level periodically.

SKILLCHECK ANSWERS—SECTION 2 (page 147)

Situation 1

c) Tell her the baby's having trouble breathing, but let the doctor give her the details. Avoid using clinical terms like ICU. If she doesn't know what that means, it may frighten or confuse her. Don't tell her not to worry or pretend that nothing's wrong.

Situation 2

b) Stop feeding Mr. Tarsky, but remain with him. Your presence may encourage and comfort him. Chances are, Mr. Tarsky has fears that he can't express readily. If you reassure him of your support, he may be able to tell you about them.

Situation 3
d) Mrs. Saunders is confused and in crisis. You can help her by turning on the lights and trying to reorient her in the ways you learned in Chapter 5. Sedation isn't always the right way to manage confusion; neither is restraint.

Situation 4
c) Listen to his complaints. Keep your own responses brief and calm. Never argue with a patient, even if you become angry. Instead, respond with behavior that's the direct opposite of his. When he complains, listen attentively. When he harasses and curses you, respond calmly and briefly.

Situation 5
d) Talk to her, including all the statements mentioned. Try to focus the conversation by repeating the patient's words. Draw her out by assuring her her feelings are not unusual and that motherhood's a big challenge. Offer to help her learn about caring for her baby.

Situation 6
f) The parents of infants who die from SIDS need assurance that it was not their fault. The exact cause of crib death is still a mystery, but the SIDS foundation can give them literature and support to help them through their grieving period.

Situation 7
e) It's important to understand the patient's needs. In this case, a facelift is not a trivial matter to Ms. White. She may need all the support you can give. Help her regain her independence by placing items within her reach. Don't exclude the family from helping in situations like this either.

Situation 8
d) Tell Mr. Royer that he's in the hospital and you're a nurse. Ask him if he remembers coming to the hospital. Never humor a confused patient. Try to reorient him as sensitively as you can. Engage him in conversation about himself. Personal events may be the easiest for him to remember.

Situation 9
d) Tell her she's in the hospital and her son, Wayne, is at home. Gently reorient the confused patient. When Mrs. Diaz understands her son's not in danger, her anxiety may decrease.

Situation 10
c) The patient who's attempted suicide may attempt it again. Try to engage him in conversation to learn what he's thinking, but don't challenge him immediately by discussing his suicide attempt. Professional counselling may be necessary, but you should be alert to his problems and consider them in your care plan.

Situation 11
c and d) Trying to form a pact with a suicidal patient can sometimes be an effective way of making him responsible to you, as well as himself. But, keep the other nurses informed of his condition. Remember, even trained professionals can't always avert suicide. But make sure you've alerted the patient's doctor about your fears.

Situation 12
d) Never ignore any warning, a patient gives that he's thinking about suicide, no matter how lightly he gives them. By removing dangerous items from the room and having a volunteer stay with him, you're minimizing the chance he'll take his life. Professional counselling will help him deal with his suicidal feelings. You can help by carefully documenting all your observations.

Situation 13
d) Don't make false promises. But don't put the patient on the defensive either. Encourage Janice to confront her parents with the fact that she attempted suicide.

Situation 14
c) Rape's an unpleasant thing to think about for most everyone. Consider the mother's feelings. Offer to sit with her before she faces her daughter and talk about it. If you help her talk about her fears, she may be able to face her daughter more easily.

Situation 15
c and d) With these signs, alcohol intoxication alone doesn't cause unconsciousness. But it could if it were mixed with barbiturates. Considering Jerry's collapse, he may also have sustained a head injury.

Situation 16
c and d) Whenever you see an unexplained injury in a child, suspect abuse. Don't assume a friend or co-worker can't be guilty of child abuse. A child's life may depend on your prompt intervention. Encourage your friend to talk about her feelings, but avoid accusing her of abusing her child. Remember, the child's injury may have been accidental.

SKILLCHECK ANSWERS—SECTION 3 (page 177)

Situation 1

a) Alice is not suffering professional burnout. Even though she expends a lot of energy on her singing avocation, she seems to love it. Chances are, she returns to work refreshed. As long as the quality of her patient care goes unaffected, Alice should continue her outside interest. A hobby or avocation is a strong defense against burnout.

b) Martha may be headed for professional burnout, because she's becoming too involved with her patients. Concern for patients is always essential to good nursing, but that doesn't mean you must treat every patient like a member of your own family. Martha's habit of working overtime, beyond the call of duty, suggests that she's sacrificing her personal life for her professional one. And if she's neglecting some of her routine duties so she'll have more time to spend with her patients, she may be contributing to a unit crisis.

c) Marie may also be headed for professional burnout, because her expectations are probably unrealistic. A supportive supervisor is a big plus. But if the hospital's plagued with funding problems, it's unlikely Marie can transform it single-handedly. As a perfectionist, she'll probably find herself assuming more and more of the other staff members' duties to make sure they're done right. To avoid burnout, she may have to reconsider her decision to stay.

Situation 2

e) Avoid confronting Sarah until you can find a private place to talk. Then, ask what you can do to help her. Answer "a" is the wrong approach, because it'll put her on the defensive. Answer "b" doesn't solve any of the unit's problems or help Sarah solve her own. Answer "c" skirts the real problem and treats only your immediate aggravation. Answer "d" is premature. Don't involve others in a problem with you and a co-worker until you've had a chance to talk about it. Answer "f" is also hasty. Why? Because Sarah may not have a drinking problem at all.

Situation 3

e) You face burnout when you start concentrating exclusively on one part of your job; you start categorizing your patients; and you regularly work overtime.

Situation 4

a) This answer is false. The unit that runs with clockwork efficiency is not immune from stressful events.

b) This answer is true. Every unit shows signs of tension.

c) This answer is false. The first sign of professional burnout in a nurse can be any number of things: indifference to patients is one, but so is overinvolvement, cynicism, and gossiping. For a complete list of burnout signs, see Chapter 10.

d) This answer is false. Competition is not the best way to ensure good patient care. Instead of helping, it divides loyalties and creates friction. Encourage teamwork instead.

e) This answer is false. The best units must have a workable blend of leaders and followers.

f) This answer is false. As a good nurse, you should never ignore your personal needs. However, that doesn't mean you should ignore your patients' needs. Try to strike a balance between the two.

INDEX

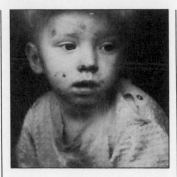

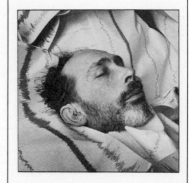

SUGGESTED FURTHER READING

Apgar, Virginia, and Joan Beck. IS MY BABY ALL RIGHT? New York, Trident Press, 1973.

Aquilera, Donna C., and Janice M. Messick. CRISIS INTERVENTION: THEORY AND METHODOLOGY, 3rd ed. St. Louis, C. V. Mosby Company, 1978.

Becker, Charles E., et al. ALCOHOL AS A DRUG: A CURRICULUM ON PHARMACOLOGY, NEUROLOGY AND TOXICOLOGY. Baltimore, Williams & Wilkins Company, 1974.

Bejerot, Nils. ADDICTION AND SOCIETY. Springfield, Charles C. Thomas Publishers, 1970.

Brown, Martha M., and Grace R. Fowler. PSYCHODYNAMIC NURSING: A BIOSOCIAL ORIENTATION, 4th ed. Philadelphia, W. B. Saunders Company, 1971.

Capean, Gerald. PRINCIPLES OF PREVENTIVE PSYCHIATRY. New York, Basic Books, Inc., 1964.

Cosgriff, James H. Jr., and Diann Anderson. THE PRACTICE OF EMERGENCY NURSING. Philadelphia, J. B. Lippincott Company, 1975.

Cull, John G., and Richard E. Hardy, eds. ALCOHOL ABUSE & REHABILITATION APPROACHES. American Lecture in Social and Rehabilitation Psychology Series. Springfield, Charles C. Thomas Publishers, 1974.

Epstein, Samuel S., and Joshua Lederberg, eds. DRUGS OF ABUSE: THEIR GENETIC AND OTHER CHRONIC NON-PSYCHIATRIC HAZARDS. Cambridge, The M.I.T. Press, 1971.

Goldenson, R. THE ENCYCLOPEDIA OF HUMAN BEHAVIOR. New York, Doubleday and Company, Inc., 1970.

Greenblatt, Milton, and Marc A. Schuckit, eds. ALCOHOLISM PROBLEMS IN WOMEN AND CHILDREN. Seminars in Psychiatry. New York, Grune & Stratton, 1976.

Hall, Calvin S., and Gardner Lindzey. THEORIES OF PERSONALITY, 2nd ed. New York, John Wiley and Sons, 1970.

Hall, Nancy. A TRUE STORY OF A DRUNKEN MOTHER. Plainfield, Daughters Publishing Company, 1974.

Helfer, Ray E., and C. Henry Kempe. THE BATTERED CHILD, 2nd ed. Chicago, University of Chicago Press, 1978.

Hore, Brian D. ALCOHOL DEPENDENCE. Woburn, Butterworths Publishing, Inc., 1976.

Jones, Dorothy A., et al. MEDICAL-SURGICAL NURSING: A CONCEPTUAL APPROACH. New York, McGraw-Hill Book Company, 1978.

Kempe, C. Henry, and Ray E. Helfer, eds. HELPING THE BATTERED CHILD AND HIS FAMILY. Philadelphia, J. B. Lippincott Company, 1972.

Kintzel, Kay C., ed. ADVANCED CONCEPTS IN CLINICAL NURSING, 2nd ed. Philadelphia, J. B. Lippincott Company, 1977.

Kyes, Joan J., and Charles K. Hofling. BASIC PSYCHIATRIC CONCEPTS IN NURSING, 3rd ed. Philadelphia, J. B. Lippincott and Company, 1974.

Luckmann, Joan, and Karen C. Sorensen. MEDICAL-SURGICAL NURSING: A PSYCHOPHYSIOLOGIC APPROACH. Philadelphia, W. B. Saunders Company, 1974.

Meyer, Roger E. GUIDE TO DRUG REHABILITATION: A PUBLIC HEALTH APPROACH. Boston, Beacon Press, 1973.

Parad, Howard J. CRISIS INTERVENTION: SELECTED READINGS. New York, Family Services Association of America, 1965.

Richter, Ralph W. MEDICAL ASPECTS OF DRUG ABUSE. Hagerstown, Harper & Row Publishers, Inc., 1975.

Robinson, Lisa. PSYCHIATRIC NURSING AS A HUMAN EXPERIENCE. Philadelphia, W. B. Saunders Company, 1977.

Rogers, Martha E. AN INTRODUCTION TO THE THEORETICAL BASIS OF NURSING. Philadelphia, F. A. Davis Company, 1970.

Selye, Hans. STRESS WITHOUT DISTRESS. New York, J. B. Lippincott Company, 1974.

Shafer, Kathleen N., et al. MEDICAL-SURGICAL NURSING, 6th ed. St. Louis, C. V. Mosby Company, 1975.

Shapte, R., and D. Lewis. THRIVE ON STRESS. New York, Warner Books, Inc., 1978.

Sproul, Carmen W., and Patrick J. Mullanney. EMERGENCY CARE: ASSESSMENT AND INTERVENTION. St. Louis, C. V. Mosby Company, 1974.

Travelbee, Joyce. INTERVENTION IN PSYCHIATRIC NURSING: PROCESS IN THE ONE-TO-ONE RELATIONSHIP. Philadelphia, F. A. Davis Company, 1969.

Wicks, Robert J. COUNSELING STRATEGIES AND INTERVENTION TECHNIQUES FOR THE HUMAN SERVICES. Philadelphia, J. B. Lippincott Company, 1977.